indoor/outdoor
BARBECUE
COOKBOOK

indoor/outdoor
BARBECUE
COOKBOOK

by June Roth

AN ESSANDESS SPECIAL EDITION
NEW YORK

INDOOR/OUTDOOR BARBECUE COOKBOOK

SBN: 671-10464-0

Published by Essandess Special Editions,
a division of Simon & Schuster, Inc.,
630 Fifth Avenue, New York, N.Y. 10020,
and on the same day in Canada
by Simon & Schuster of Canada, Ltd., Richmond Hill, Ontario.
PRINTED IN THE U.S.A.

Cover photo by Irwin Horowitz,
courtesy of American Express

In memory of my brother
Albert Spiewak, who had an incomparable
indoor charm and outdoor zest for living.

Contents

indoor/outdoor
BARBECUE
COOKBOOK

1/ Barbecue Skills

Ever since man accidentally discovered that fire added warmth and finger-licking happiness to his dinner, cooks through the centuries have devised methods of barbecuing almost every kind of food into succulent offerings. Now, as never before, the assortment of indoor and outdoor cooking equipment and the best foods of the world's markets is available to you. With these advantages, and with your careful study, barbecuing can become an exciting part of your cooking repertoire.

Half the secret—and the fun—of a good barbecue lies in the preparations you make, preparations that begin even before you strike a match.

The first secret of outdoor cooking success is a good bed of coals. Start preparing it almost one hour before you want to cook. If your grill is portable, put it in a shielded area; line the bottom with heavy aluminum foil to reflect the heat; and arrange the briquets on the foil. Start the fire with a commercial fire-starting gel, or liquid, or one of the newer fire-starting packets. Let it burn for about thirty minutes, until the briquets look gray and flameless. If you rush to cook over the flames—no matter how glorious they look—you risk the chance of burning the food. Gray, ashy-looking briquets may look less dramatic, but are actually filled with intense heat which cooks evenly and dependably.

Secondly, it is important to know how to arrange the charcoal so that the fire is not directly under the food. This is especially necessary for meat and poultry that require a long cooking time. The drippings from such barbecues often cause high flames that char rather than cook. To avoid such culinary pitfalls, arrange the charcoal to give indirect heat. You can either mound it in the center of the grill and plan to cook the meat around the outside of the fire, or you can arrange the coals on one side of the grill and cook on the other. One of the most direct advantages to this indirect heat grilling is that it requires less attention from the chef.

The third secret that every successful barbecuer must learn is the importance of "marinating"—that is, of soaking meat or other foods in a mixture (the "marinade") that will provide extra tenderness and flavor. Many recipes in this book call for marinating to help prevent the meat from drying out during the cooking period. Observe the time allowances for this process and you will add a bonus to your meals.

Gather the right equipment for safety and efficiency; make sure your tools have long handles and that you have asbestos gloves and potholders handy. Keep a roll of heavy-duty aluminum foil to cover food or to make pans for cooking or for drippings.

Barbecue gear itself can be simple or elaborate, depending on your space and taste. Preferably, the grill should have a movable rack so its distance from the fire can be adjusted. A fire pan with holes will allow for circulation of air through the coals. Two-sided broiling racks are a good investment for keeping small items together and making them easy to handle. Just a turn of the rack and a handful of frankfurters can be toasted on both sides and removed at one time. Gas-fired ceramic coal units are gaining popularity since they are easy and efficient to use and will not detract from the taste of your barbecue. A battery- or electric-powered rotisserie is a great asset to the barbecue chef, making trussed poultry and beef roasts an easy possibility.

All good cooks know that you are only as good as your recipes, and here is a special collection of barbecue recipes, each unique in taste and easy to prepare. All of these recipes can be adapted to the indoor barbecue pit, range broiler, rotisserie, or oven, while retaining their special marinated flavors. Barbecuing need not be only a summertime treat. It's also a way of bringing in summer tastes to cheer up tiresome winter cooking. So grab your chef's hat as boss of the grill, and take note of the many ways you can fire up your cooking —and the appetites of your family and friends—with these hearty recipes!

2/Hot Appetizers

Hunger pangs seem to get a gnawing head start when people are standing around the grill watching their dinner barbecue to perfection. It's a good time to have a small hibachi cooking up some appetizing tidbits until the entree is ready, or to make room on the dinner grill for a few tasty snacks.

Bear in mind, too, that the word "barbecue" evokes the

rugged outdoors, no matter where the food is actually cooked, so start your guests and family off to a nibbling good time by preparing—ahead of time—taste-teasers that can be picked up with the fingers in gay abandon of dining room manners. What better way to wish all those around you a hearty appetite than by providing a spread of hearty appetizers!

RUMAKI

12 water chestnuts, cut in 4 slices
12 chicken livers, cut in quarters
12 slices bacon, cut in fourths

½ cup soy sauce
½ cup dry sherry
2 teaspoons brown sugar
½ teaspoon ginger

OUTDOORS   Place a slice of water chestnut next to a chicken liver quarter and wrap part of a slice of bacon around them; fasten with toothpicks. After assembling 48 such appetizers, combine soy sauce, sherry, sugar, and ginger, preferably in a small plastic bag set in a bowl. Place fastened appetizers in this marinade and fasten plastic bag securely; refrigerate for several hours, turning bag frequently to redistribute marinade. To cook, place on hibachi or outdoor grill for about 5 minutes. Serve hot.

INDOORS   Cook under broiler for about 5 minutes.
Makes 4 dozen appetizers.

EASY STEAMED CLAMS WITH PEPPERY BUTTER DIP

1 (3-pound) can steamed clams in the shell
½ pound butter, melted

1 lemon, cut in 8 wedges
Hot red pepper sauce (commercially prepared)

OUTDOORS   Remove top of clam can and heat clams in this container right on the grill. When hot, remove clams from broth, reserving broth. To eat, detach the clam from the shell with your fingers, holding it by its long neck. Swish the clam in the broth to wash off any lingering grains of sand, then dip it into individual bowls that contain a mixture of melted butter, juice of a lemon wedge, and hot red pepper sauce to taste. Bite off the succulent soft portion; use the black collar as a handle and discard. When you have finished the clams, you may want to sip the hot clam broth, but be sure to leave the last dregs, which contain the sandy residue.

INDOORS   Pour contents of clam can into saucepan and heat on range. Continue as above.
Makes 8 appetizer servings.

LITTLE RUBIES

1 (1-pound, 5-ounce) can cherry pie filling
1 cup rosé wine

1 pound cocktail frankfurters, cut in half

Empty cherry pie filling into a chafing dish and add rosé wine. Heat slowly for about 5 minutes. Add miniature wieners and heat to serving temperature. Keep warm in chafing dish over low flame. Use long picks for serving.
Makes 32 appetizers.

COCKTAIL FRANKS IN CURRANT-MUSTARD SAUCE

1 pound cocktail frankfurters

1 (10-ounce) jar currant jelly
1 cup prepared mustard

Place frankfurters in water; bring to a boil. Remove from heat and let stand 5 minutes; drain. Melt currant jelly over low heat; add mustard and stir until blended. Keep warm until serving time, or reheat on the edge of grill just before serving. Add frankfurters. Use a chafing dish to keep frankfurters and sauce hot. Serve with tiny slices of rye bread or melba toast. *Makes about 2 dozen hot hors d'oeuvres.*

STUFFED COCKTAIL FRANKS

1 (4¾-ounce) can liverwurst spread	2 tablespoons chopped fresh parsley
½ cup crushed cheese crackers	24 small cocktail frankfurters

OUTDOORS Combine liverwurst spread, crackers, and parsley. Slit each frankfurter lengthwise, but not all the way through, and fill it with about 1½ teaspoons of the liver mixture. Grill about 5 inches from heat until browned. Serve immediately.

INDOORS Use broiler.
Makes 24 stuffed franks.

HOT DOG TIDBITS

2 cups packaged cornflake crumbs	5 frankfurters
	⅓ cup catsup

OUTDOORS Empty cornflake crumbs into a bowl. Cut frankfurters into ¾-inch slices. Dip each slice in catsup; then roll in cornflake crumbs until well coated. Place in foil-lined shallow baking pan. Do not crowd. Heat on the grill for 20 minutes. Insert toothpicks and serve hot on appetizer trays with a dunking bowl of catsup or mustard.

INDOORS Put pan of frankfurters in a 350-degree oven for about 15 minutes.
Makes about 3 dozen appetizers.

HIBACHI WIENERS

2 pounds cocktail frankfurters

OUTDOORS Cook frankfurters on grill.

INDOORS Cook frankfurters under broiler.

Serve with one of the following sauces:

Creamy Mustard Sauce
½ pint dairy sour cream
1 tablespoon instant minced onion

1 tablespoon prepared mustard
2 teaspoons steak sauce
½ teaspoon salt

Blend ingredients and chill.
Makes about 1 cup.

Barbecue Sauce
1 (8-ounce) can tomato sauce
2 tablespoons prepared mustard

½ teaspoon Worcestershire sauce
¼ teaspoon ground cloves

Combine ingredients in small saucepan. Heat 5 minutes and serve.
Makes about 1 cup.

18

Hibachi Wieners with Creamy Mustard Sauce, Barbecue Sauce, and Peach-Orange Sauce

For a tasty appetizer, cook up some cocktail franks on the grill or under the broiler and let your guests dip them in flavorful sauces. Sausages and pineapple and green pepper chunks can be grilled at the same time and dipped in sauce. Use plastic food picks for dunking. Courtesy of Oscar Mayer & Company

Peach-Orange Sauce

1 (1-pound) can peaches	¼ cup sugar
⅓ cup water	½ teaspoon ginger
½ orange, cut in pieces	⅛ teaspoon salt
2 tablespoons cornstarch	

Drain peaches, reserving ⅔ cup juice. Cut peaches in pieces and combine with reserved juice, water, and orange in saucepan. Cook 5 minutes. Combine cornstarch, sugar, ginger, and salt; add to peach mixture and cook until glossy.
Makes about 2 cups.

FRENCH BACON DIP

1 (½-pound) package
sliced bacon
1 (8-ounce) package
cream cheese

½ cup dairy sour cream
⅓ cup Thousand Island
dressing
⅓ cup dry white wine

OUTDOORS   Cut bacon into 1-inch pieces. Cook in pan or on aluminum foil on grill until crisp; drain. Blend together cream cheese, sour cream, and Thousand Island dressing. Add wine and stir until smooth. Chill. Stir in bacon pieces just before serving. Serve with crackers or chips or fresh vegetable spears.

INDOORS   Cook bacon in skillet on range.
Makes 2 cups.

CHIP CHEESE BALLS

½ cup grated raw carrot
½ cup finely crushed
potato chips

1 (3-ounce) package cream
cheese, softened
½ cup chopped parsley

Mix grated carrots and crushed potato chips with soft cream cheese. Shape into 1-inch balls. Roll in chopped parsley. Chill before serving.
Makes about 1 dozen cheese balls.

BANANA SURPRISE

3 large ripe bananas   1 teaspoon vanilla
½ cup dairy sour cream   1 cup shredded coconut

Peel and cut bananas in chunks about 1 inch thick. Combine sour cream with vanilla, mixing well. Dip each piece of banana in sour cream and roll in coconut. Chill.
Makes about 16 appetizers.

HERBED POTATO CHIPS

1 package fresh potato   Thyme
  chips   Paprika
  Marjoram

OUTDOORS   Spread potato chips in shallow pan; sprinkle lightly with marjoram and thyme. Place on the grill for 20 minutes. Remove from heat and sprinkle generously with paprika.

INDOORS   Heat potato chips in a 250-degree oven for 20 minutes.

3/ Simmering, Shimmering Soups

Some like it hot. Some like it cold. However you prefer it, soup is a welcome addition to any barbecue.

Think of a pot of bouillon simmering on the edge of the grill, ready to be ladled into deep mugs for casual sipping. Or a cool shimmering madrilène that soothes away the effects of a high-humidity day.

Don't forget the soup-toppers: bits of chives, parsley, thin lemon slices, garlic-flavored croutons, or anything else you can think of that will add a dash of glamour to the brew. And do remember that soup has a hospitality all its own.

In this chapter you will find a collection of hot and cold offerings that can be counted on to give a good taste performance at every barbecue. You will be ladling out soup and gathering in compliments to your heart's content.

SPICY WARM-UP

1 (24-ounce) can V-8 juice
1 tablespoon brown sugar
1 teaspoon lemon juice
Dash of allspice
Dash of cinnamon

OUTDOORS In a saucepan, combine V-8 juice, sugar, lemon juice, allspice, and cinnamon. Heat on the grill. Pour into mugs, with a cinnamon stick for swizzling if desired.

INDOORS Heat soup on range.
Makes 6 servings.

FISHERMAN'S CHOWDER

¼ pound bacon, finely chopped
6 cups water
1 (14½-ounce) can evaporated milk
3 tablespoons instant minced onion
1 teaspoon salt
½ teaspoon black pepper
2 pounds boneless fish fillets
1 (5-serving) envelope instant mashed potato granules

OUTDOORS Cook bacon in a large saucepan on the grill until golden brown and crisp and drain. Add water, milk, onion, salt, and pepper; bring to a boil. Cut fish into small pieces (about 1 inch square) and add to liquid. Simmer about 10 minutes until fish is done. Stir in instant potato directly from the envelope. Serve piping hot.

INDOORS   Cook on range.
Makes 8 servings.

Fisherman's Chowder

Simmer fish chunks in a savory liquid, add instant mashed potatoes at the last minute, and you'll have a rich, thick chowder like this one. Serve it hot, with crisp crackers. Courtesy of R. T. French Company

TUNA CHOWDER

2 (7-ounce) cans tuna in vegetable oil
1 medium onion, sliced
1 (10½-ounce) can condensed cream of celery soup
1 cup beer or ale
1 (1-pound) can cream-style corn

3 cups milk
⅛ teaspoon basil
¼ teaspoon Tabasco sauce
½ teaspoon celery salt
2 pimientos, chopped
1 tablespoon chopped parsley

OUTDOORS   Drain tuna oil into deep kettle. Add sliced onion and cook until tender but not brown. Stir in condensed cream of celery soup; blend in beer. Add tuna, corn, milk, basil, Tabasco sauce, and celery salt. Place kettle on grill and simmer for 10 minutes. Add pimientos and parsley. Serve hot.

INDOORS   Use range.
Makes 6–8 servings.

BEEFY BEAN SOUP

1 (15½-ounce) can kidney beans, drained and rinsed in cold water
1 (10½-ounce) can condensed vegetable-beef soup

1 tablespoon red port wine
1 soup can of water
¼ teaspoon oregano

OUTDOORS   Combine beans, soup, wine, water, and oregano in a saucepan. Stir. Heat mixture thoroughly on grill. Serve piping hot.

INDOORS   Use range.
Makes 4 servings.

TOMATO-BEAN SOUP

1 (1-pound) can baked
beans
1 (10½-ounce) can
condensed tomato soup
1 soup can of water

1 fresh tomato, cut in
small pieces
2 strips bacon, cooked
and crumbled

OUTDOORS   Combine beans, tomato soup, water, and tomato in a saucepan. Stir. Heat on the grill. Serve hot, topped with crumbled bacon.

INDOORS   Heat soup on range.
Makes 4 servings.

TOMATO-DILL SOUP

1 quart tomato juice
2 tablespoons butter
1 teaspoon Worcestershire
sauce

¼ teaspoon pepper
1 teaspoon ground dill
Popcorn balls

OUTDOORS   Combine all ingredients, except popcorn balls, in a large saucepan and heat on the edge of a hot grill. Ladle into large mugs and garnish with popcorn balls.

INDOORS   Heat soup on range.
Makes 4 servings.

CONSOMMÉ BELLEVUE

2½ cups clam broth
1 (10½-ounce) can
condensed consommé

1 tablespoon minced dill

OUTDOORS Heat clam broth with consommé and minced dill in saucepan on grill. Serve piping hot in bouillon cups.

INDOORS Use range.
Makes 4 servings.

MINT VELVET

1 (11¼-ounce) can condensed green pea soup
1 soup can of water
1 (10½-ounce) can condensed consommé

1 tablespoon white wine (optional)
¼ teaspoon chopped mint leaves
Popcorn balls

OUTDOORS Empty green pea soup into a saucepan; gradually stir in water. Add consommé, wine, and mint leaves. Heat on the grill. Serve in mugs, topped with popcorn balls.

INDOORS Heat on range.
Makes 4 servings.

CREAMY CELERY-NOODLE SOUP

⅓ cup very thinly sliced carrots
1½ cups water
1 (10½-ounce) can condensed cream of celery soup

1 (10½-ounce) can condensed beef-noodle soup
½ soup can of milk
Minced parsley

OUTDOORS In covered saucepan, cook carrots in water over low heat until tender, about 5–7 minutes. Gradually blend in celery soup. Add beef-noodle soup and milk. Heat over grill, stirring now and then. Garnish with parsley and serve in heavy mugs.

INDOORS   Heat soup on range.
Makes 4–6 servings.

SEASIDE GAZPACHO

1 (16-ounce) can Clamato juice
1 (15-ounce) jar stewed tomatoes
1 slice white bread, crumbled
½ cup garlic-flavored salad dressing

1 cucumber, chopped
1 large Bermuda onion, chopped
1 large green pepper, diced
1 cup packaged garlic-flavored croutons

Place Clamato juice, stewed tomatoes, crumbled bread, and dressing in a bowl. Beat together, then chill for 1 hour. Before serving, beat again, or whirl in blender for several seconds. Divide cucumber, onion, and green pepper into 6 bowls and pour juice mixture over each. Top with croutons.
Makes 6 servings.

SPARKLE-UP SOUP

1 (10½-ounce) can condensed beef broth
½ cup club soda

Ice cubes
Lemon twists

In a pitcher, combine beef broth and soda. Pour over ice cubes in a glass. Garnish with a twist of lemon.
Makes 3–4 servings.

TOMATO FIZZ

1 (10¾-ounce) can
   condensed tomato soup
1 cup cold water

⅓ cup lemon-lime soda
Grated lemon rind

Place soup in refrigerator for 3–4 hours. Combine soup and water; stir in soda. Serve in chilled mugs with a garnish of lemon rind.
Makes 2–3 servings.

JELLIED CLAM MADRILÈNE

1 (16-ounce) can Clamato
   juice
1 package unflavored
   gelatin

½ tablespoon lemon juice
¼ cup chopped scallions

Empty juice into saucepan; stir in gelatin to soften, then heat and stir to dissolve completely. Add lemon juice. Chill until slightly thickened. Pour into shallow pan, or loaf pan, rinsed in cold water. Chill until firm. Cut into strips and serve in sherbet dishes. Top with chopped scallions.
Makes 4 servings.

AVOCADO MADRILÈNE

1 (16-ounce) can Clamato
   juice
1 package unflavored
   gelatin
½ tablespoon lemon juice

1 small avocado, pureed
¼ cup dairy sour cream
2 tablespoons chopped
   chives

29

Empty juice into a saucepan; stir in gelatin to soften, then heat and stir to dissolve completely. Add lemon juice. Chill until slightly thickened. Pour into a shallow pan, rinsed in cold water. Chill until firm. Break up with a fork and beat slightly; add pureed avocado. Spoon into serving bowls and garnish with a spoonful of sour cream and sprinkling of chopped chives.
Makes 4 servings.

CHILLED CLAM BISQUE

1 (8-ounce) can minced clams
1 (3-ounce) package cream cheese

1 (16-ounce) can tomato juice
1 tablespoon minced chives

Combine minced clams (with broth) and cream cheese; beat until well blended. Add tomato juice. Chill. Sprinkle each serving with minced chives.
Makes 4 servings.

4/Barbecued Beef

There is something about the mixture of smoke and savory sauce that whets the appetite. Barbecue sauce changes plain beef into a moist and tantalizing feast.

On the ranch, cooks pride themselves on their special barbecue sauces, often mixed in a pail and brushed on a side of beef with a thick paintbrush or dishmop. Sometimes their zealously guarded recipes bring them fame in the surrounding countryside. But you don't have to live on a southwest prairie to enjoy the authentic taste of barbecued beef.

Here is an assortment of beef recipes, from the humble burger to the skewered kabob, from a simple steak to a wine and mushroom roast—all designed to glow in your memory long after the last morsel is eaten and the last coal burns out.

SHORT RIBS HAWAIIAN

6 pounds lean beef short ribs
1 (1-pound, 13-ounce) can pineapple slices
½ cup soy sauce
½ cup honey
1 cup water
1 tablespoon prepared mustard
2 tablespoons brown sugar
1 clove garlic, minced
1 teaspoon ginger

OUTDOORS   Arrange beef ribs in a small flat pan. Top with pineapple slices. Combine 1⅓ cups pineapple syrup from slices, soy sauce, honey, water, mustard, sugar, garlic, and ginger in a saucepan; simmer for 5 minutes. Pour over beef ribs and refrigerate for several hours. When ready to grill, remove ribs and pineapple slices from sauce; place ribs on a hot grill and cook for 25–30 minutes, basting often with the sauce and turning often to prevent burning. Place pineapple slices on grill for 5 minutes before serving.

INDOORS   Roast ribs in a 375-degree oven, basting as above. Broil pineapple slices just before serving.
Makes 6–8 servings.

WINE AND MUSHROOM CHUCK ROAST

3- to 4-pound chuck roast, 2 inches thick
1 (¾-ounce) envelope mushroom gravy mix
½ cup dry red wine

OUTDOORS Place chuck roast on two sheets of heavy-duty aluminum foil. Sprinkle meat with contents of gravy-mix envelope; turn up sides of foil and pour wine over meat. Wrap securely in foil, using double folds. Place on grill; cook 2–3 hours or until done.

INDOORS Place wrapped roast in a pan and cook in a 350-degree oven for 2 hours.
Makes 6–8 servings.

Wine and Mushroom Chuck Roast

This succulent roast is surprisingly easy to prepare. Cover the meat with mushroom gravy mix and red wine and wrap it securely in foil. After cooking unattended for several hours, the roast will be juicy and tender. Serve with baked potatoes, a crisp green salad, and French bread for a simple but elegant meal.
Courtesy of R. T. French Company

BEEF KABOBS

2 pounds top or bottom round of beef, cut in cubes
Instant meat tenderizer
6 small onions, parboiled 5 minutes

1 medium green pepper, parboiled 2 minutes, cut in squares
12 cherry tomatoes
Olive oil

OUTDOORS   Thoroughly moisten the surface of the meat with water; sprinkle instant meat tenderizer evenly, like salt, over the entire surface of the meat. Thread meat cubes on skewers alternately with onions, green pepper, and tomatoes, using about 4 cubes of meat on each. Brush kabobs with olive oil and place on grill about 2 inches from hot coals. Cook 5–6 minutes for rare, 6–8 minutes for medium, turning frequently.

INDOORS   Cook under broiler.
Makes 6 servings.

BEEF AND CORN KABOBS

1 cup salad oil
¼ cup cider vinegar
3 tablespoons prepared yellow mustard
1½ teaspoons garlic salt
½ teaspoon black pepper
1½ pounds boneless sirloin steak, about ¾ inch thick

6 medium onions
2 green peppers
3 ears of corn
1 dozen medium-size mushrooms

OUTDOORS   Make a marinade by combining in a saucepan the salad oil, vinegar, mustard, garlic salt, and pepper. Heat mixture to boiling; cool. Cut steak into 1½-inch squares; cut onions in half crosswise, and cut each pepper into 8 or 12 pieces. Place meat and cut vegetables in a shallow pan and pour marinade over them; stir gently so all pieces are well coated. Cover; let stand in refrigerator 4–6 hours or overnight. Cut each ear of corn into 4 or 5 pieces. Wash mushrooms. Make kabobs by alternating pieces of meat and vegetables on skewers; baste kabobs with remaining marinade. Grill over charcoal fire for 20–25 minutes or until done, turning skewers and basting frequently.

INDOORS Place skewers in a 350-degree oven for 30 minutes, basting as above.
Makes 6 servings.

BARBECUED BREAKFAST STEAKS SAMURAI

9 cube steaks, 1/4 inch thick	2 tablespoons soy sauce
1 package instant meat marinade	1 tablespoon molasses
1/4 teaspoon ginger	2/3 cup cold water
1/4 teaspoon dry mustard	1 clove garlic, minced
	Watercress

OUTDOORS Cut each breakfast steak in half. Pour contents of package of meat marinade into a shallow pan. Thoroughly blend in ginger, mustard, soy sauce, molasses, water, and garlic. Place meat in marinade. Turn meat and thoroughly pierce all surfaces with a fork. Marinate 15 minutes, turning several times. Remove meat; reserve marinade. Using three skewers, lace 3 pieces of steak on each. Place on barbecue grill set 1 inch above hot coals. Grill about 1 minute on each side. Baste frequently with extra marinade. To serve, remove meat from skewers and add a garnish of watercress.

INDOORS Use broiler.
Makes 6 servings.

TERIYAKI

2 pounds sirloin steak, about 1 inch thick
1/3 cup chopped onion
1 teaspoon ginger
1/2 cup soy sauce
1/4 cup sherry
1/3 cup unsulphured molasses
1 (1-pound) can pineapple chunks, drained

OUTDOORS   Cut steak into 1-inch cubes. Combine onion, ginger, soy sauce, sherry, and molasses in a bowl; mix well. Add meat. Cover and refrigerate several hours or overnight. Remove meat. Alternate meat on skewers with pineapple chunks. Grill until done.

INDOORS   Use broiler.
Makes 6 servings.

BARBECUED FLANK STEAK

1 flank steak, about 2½ pounds
1 onion, finely chopped
1/2 teaspoon mustard
1/2 teaspoon salt
1/2 teaspoon dried leaf basil
1/4 teaspoon Tabasco sauce
1 clove garlic, crushed
1/4 cup oil
Tomato wedges
Green pepper squares
Onions, parboiled
Mushroom caps

OUTDOORS   Place flank steak in shallow pan. Combine onion, mustard, salt, basil, Tabasco sauce, garlic, and oil; pour over steak and let marinate 4 hours or longer. Remove steak from marinade. Grill about 5 minutes on each side for medium rare or until done as desired. Meanwhile, skewer vegetables; brush with marinade and barbecue during last 5 minutes of steak cooking time. Slice steak on the diagonal across the grain to serve.

INDOORS   Use broiler.
Makes 4–6 servings.

GOLD RUSH STEAK

¼ cup prepared mustard
1 tablespoon sugar
1 tablespoon instant
   minced onion
2 tablespoons
   Worcestershire sauce
1 tablespoon catsup
1½ teaspoons salt

⅛ teaspoon garlic powder
⅛ teaspoon cayenne
½ pound butter or
   margarine, softened
2 sirloin steaks, about
   4 pounds each,
   2 inches thick

OUTDOORS Combine mustard, sugar, onion, Worcestershire sauce, catsup, salt, garlic powder, and cayenne. Add gradually to softened butter, mixing thoroughly. Grill steaks on one side for 15 minutes, turn, spread cooked sides with ½ the butter mixture. When other sides are done, spread them with remaining mixture.

INDOORS Cook under broiler.
Makes 12 or more servings.

GOURMET GRILLED STEAK

½ teaspoon dry mustard
½ teaspoon water
2 tablespoons
   Worcestershire sauce
2 tablespoons butter,
   melted

1 (2- to 3-pound) sirloin
   steak
Salt
Pepper

OUTDOORS Mix mustard with water; let stand 10 minutes. Combine with Worcestershire sauce and butter. Grill steak on one side, turn and make several shallow slashes across top of steak. Pour butter mixture over steak and complete grilling. Season to taste with salt and pepper.

INDOORS Cook under broiler.
Makes 4–6 servings.

STEAK WITH MUSHROOM SAUCE

4 club steaks, cut 1½
  inches thick
Salt
Pepper
¼ cup butter

Juice of ½ lemon
1 (2½-ounce) jar sliced
  mushrooms, drained
1 tablespoon minced parsley

OUTDOORS Grill steaks 3–5 inches from coals about 20 minutes, turning once. To test for doneness, cut a small slit in meat and check color. Season lightly with salt and pepper just before removing from grill. While steaks are cooking, combine butter, lemon juice, mushrooms, and parsley in small saucepan. Heat near edge of grill until butter is melted. Spoon over hot steaks.

INDOORS Cook steak under broiler. Heat mushroom sauce on range.
Makes 4 servings.

GREAT STEAK

1 porterhouse or sirloin
  steak, about 3 pounds
2 teaspoons monosodium
  glutamate

½ teaspoon salt
¼ teaspoon pepper
2 teaspoons prepared
  mustard

OUTDOORS Trim excess fat from steak. Slash fat edge to prevent curling. Season steak with monosodium glutamate, salt, and pepper; rub in well. Spread prepared mustard over surface. Grill to desired degree of doneness, turning once.

INDOORS Cook under broiler.
Makes 4–6 servings.

LONDON BROIL WITH MUSTARD BUTTER

2 flank steaks, about 1½   ¼ teaspoon pepper
   pounds each   ¼ cup prepared mustard
½ teaspoon salt   ¼ cup butter, softened

OUTDOORS Slash steak on edges to prevent curling during cooking. Season with salt and pepper. Combine mustard and butter and heat in a saucepan on the edge of the grill. Brush steaks with ½ of the butter mixture; place on grill so that steak is about 3 inches from heat. Cook about 6 minutes on each side for medium rare. Do not overcook as meat will toughen. To serve, slice very thinly on a diagonal, across the grain. Pour remaining butter sauce over carved meat.

INDOORS Heat butter mixture on range. Cook steak under broiler.
Makes 6–8 servings.

BARBECUED MEAT LOAF

¼ cup unsulphured   ¼ cup finely chopped
   molasses   parsley
¼ cup prepared mustard   1 tablespoon salt
¼ cup vinegar   ½ teaspoon thyme
1 cup tomato juice   3 pounds ground beef
2 eggs   1 (1-pound, 14-ounce)
3 cups soft bread crumbs   can peach halves
1 medium onion, finely
   chopped

OUTDOORS Blend molasses and prepared mustard; stir in vinegar. Add ½ cup of mixture to tomato juice and eggs in large mixing bowl; beat until blended. Stir in bread crumbs, onion, parsley, salt, and thyme. Add ground beef; mix well.

Form into loaf in a shallow baking pan. Brush with part of remaining molasses mixture. Form loose cover of aluminum foil over pan and cook on grill for 1½ hours, brushing occasionally with molasses mixture for glaze. Drain peach halves; brush with molasses mixture; add to pan 15 minutes before end of cooking time.

INDOORS Leave pan uncovered. Bake in a moderate oven (350 degrees) for 1½ hours, brushing as above.
Makes 12 servings.

HAMBURGERS WITH BARBECUE SAUCE

2 tablespoons butter	¼ cup vinegar
¼ cup finely chopped onion	¼ cup prepared mustard
½ cup unsulphured molasses	2 tablespoons Worcestershire sauce
½ cup catsup	¼ teaspoon Tabasco sauce
	3 pounds ground beef

OUTDOORS Melt butter in saucepan. Add onion and cook until tender, but not brown. Stir in remaining ingredients, except beef. Bring to a boil. Reduce heat and simmer 10 minutes. Form beef into patties. Place hamburgers on grill and baste with barbecue sauce during grilling.

INDOORS Cook hamburgers under broiler.
Makes 12 servings.

BEET BURGERS

2 pounds ground beef	1 egg, slightly beaten
1 (1-pound) jar pickled beets, chopped fine	½ teaspoon salt
1 small onion, grated	½ cup bread crumbs

OUTDOORS   Combine ground beef, chopped beets, and grated onion. Add beaten egg, salt, and bread crumbs. Mix only long enough to blend ingredients thoroughly. Form into 8 large, oval-shaped, thick rolls. Chill until ready to use. Grill over hot coals for about 5 minutes on each side or until done to taste.

INDOORS   Cook under broiler.
Makes 8 servings.

SLUMGULLION

2 tablespoons olive oil	1 teaspoon Worcestershire
1 large onion, chopped	sauce
1 pound ground beef	½ teaspoon salt
1 (8-ounce) can tomato	¼ teaspoon pepper
sauce	6 hamburger rolls

OUTDOORS   Heat oil in a skillet on the grill; sauté onion until golden. Add ground beef and break into particles with a fork as it cooks. Add tomato sauce, Worcestershire sauce, salt, and pepper. Simmer and stir for about 15 minutes; spoon over heated hamburger rolls to serve.

INDOORS   Cook in skillet on range.
Makes 6 servings.

CHEDDAR-FILLED HAMBURGERS

2 pounds ground beef	8 teaspoons pickle relish
4 teaspoons prepared	½ teaspoon salt
mustard	¼ teaspoon pepper
8 slices cheddar cheese	8 hamburger rolls

OUTDOORS Divide ground beef into 8 portions. Divide each portion into 2 thin patties, about 4 inches in diameter. Spread one patty with ½ teaspoon prepared mustard. Place slice of cheddar cheese (folded if necessary) in center of patty and spoon on 1 teaspoon pickle relish. Top with second patty, pressing edges of the patties together. Grill on each side for several minutes. Sprinkle lightly with salt and pepper. Serve on warm hamburger rolls.

INDOORS Use broiler.
Makes 8 servings.

CUCUMBURGERS

2 medium cucumbers	1 egg, slightly beaten
3 tablespoons mayonnaise	¼ cup milk
⅛ teaspoon garlic salt	1½ pounds ground beef
1¾ teaspoons salt	½ cup finely chopped
⅜ teaspoon pepper	onion
3 cups ready-to-eat high-protein cereal	8 hamburger buns, sliced and buttered

OUTDOORS Scrub cucumbers; do not peel. Grate coarsely; press in strainer to remove excess moisture. Add mayonnaise, garlic salt, ¼ teaspoon salt, and ¼ teaspoon pepper; mix thoroughly. Set aside. Combine cereal, egg, milk, ground beef, onion, and remaining salt and pepper. Shape into 8 patties. Grill about 5 minutes on each side until done. Serve on warm buttered buns; top each burger with 2 tablespoons of cucumber mixture.

INDOORS Cook under broiler.
Makes 8 servings.

ONION—RELISH-FILLED HAMBURGERS

2 pounds ground beef	8 teaspoons pickle relish
4 teaspoons prepared mustard	½ teaspoon salt
8 thin slices onion	¼ teaspoon pepper
	8 hamburger rolls

OUTDOORS Divide ground beef into 8 portions. Divide each portion into 2 thin patties, about 4 inches in diameter. Spread one patty with about ½ teaspoon mustard. Place a thin slice of onion in center. Add a teaspoon of pickle relish. Top with second patty, pressing edges of the patties together. Grill on each side for several minutes. Sprinkle lightly with salt and pepper. Serve on warm hamburger rolls.

INDOORS Use broiler.
Makes 8 servings.

ROQUEFORT-FILLED HAMBURGERS

2 pounds ground beef	½ teaspoon salt
¼ cup butter	¼ teaspoon pepper
¼ cup Roquefort cheese	8 hamburger rolls
1 tablespoon prepared mustard	

OUTDOORS Divide ground beef into 8 portions. Divide each portion into 2 thin patties, about 4 inches in diameter. Cream together the butter, cheese, and mustard. Spread about a tablespoon of this mixture on the first patty. Top with the second, pressing edges together to seal. Grill on each side for several minutes. Sprinkle lightly with salt and pepper. Serve on warm hamburger rolls.

INDOORS Use broiler.
Makes 8 servings.

Patio Patties

For hamburgers with a tasty surprise, put slices of tomato and onion between two thin patties and press their edges together. Be sure to seal burgers tightly so they will retain their shape while cooking. They are served here with hamburger buns and Herb-Roasted Corn. Courtesy of Accent International

PATIO PATTIES

1 pound ground beef
1 teaspoon monosodium
   glutamate
¾ teaspoon salt

¼ teaspoon pepper
4 thin tomato slices
4 thin onion slices

OUTDOORS Break up meat with fork in mixing bowl. Sprinkle with monosodium glutamate, salt, and pepper. Toss gently with fork to distribute ingredients. Shape into 8 thin patties. Top 4 of the patties with tomato and onion slices; cover with remaining 4 patties and press edges together to seal. Grill, turning once, until done to taste.

INDOORS Cook under broiler or panbroil.
Makes 4 servings.

BURGUNDY BURGERS

1½ pounds ground beef
½ teaspoon salt
⅛ teaspoon pepper
¼ cup Burgundy wine

2 tablespoons butter
2 tablespoons
   Worcestershire sauce

OUTDOORS Combine ground beef, salt, pepper, and wine in a bowl, mixing lightly with a fork. Shape into 6 patties. Combine butter and Worcestershire sauce in a hot skillet on the grill; add meat patties. Cook for about 10 minutes, turning to brown both sides.

INDOORS Cook in skillet on range.
Makes 6 servings.

APPLE FRANKIES

1 (7-ounce) package herb-
   seasoned stuffing
   croutons
2 cups canned apple sauce
½ cup crumbled cooked
   bacon

1 teaspoon prepared
   mustard
1 tablespoon minced
   onion
¾ cup boiling water
10 frankfurters

OUTDOORS   In a large bowl, mix croutons, apple sauce, bacon, mustard, and onion. Add boiling water and mix well. The stuffing should be moist enough to hold its shape when a small amount is pressed into a ball, so add a little more water if necessary. Slit frankfurter and press about ⅓ cup stuffing into it. Chill until ready to use. To barbecue, place frankfurters on grill for about 20 minutes.

INDOORS   Place frankfurters on a greased baking sheet and bake in a 400-degree oven for 20 minutes.
Makes 10 servings.

CONEY ISLAND HOT DOGS

¼ pound ground beef
1 (6-ounce) can tomato paste
1½ cups water
¼ cup pickle relish
1 tablespoon instant minced onion
1 tablespoon Worcestershire sauce
1 tablespoon prepared mustard
2 teaspoons chili powder
1½ teaspoons salt
1 teaspoon sugar
1 dozen frankfurters
1 dozen frankfurter rolls

OUTDOORS   Cook ground beef in a medium-size saucepan on the edge of grill, stirring to break up meat into small particles. Add tomato paste, water, relish, onion, Worcestershire sauce, mustard, chili powder, salt, and sugar. Simmer 30 minutes, stirring occasionally. Makes about 2 cups of sauce, enough to spoon over 1 dozen grilled frankfurters on rolls.

INDOORS   Make sauce in saucepan on range. Cook frankfurters under broiler and warm rolls in the oven.
Makes 12 servings.

FRANKFURTERS WITH BARBECUE SAUCE

2 tablespoons butter
¼ cup finely chopped onion
½ cup unsulphured molasses
½ cup chili sauce
¼ cup lemon juice
¼ cup prepared mustard
2 tablespoons Worcestershire sauce
¼ teaspoon Tabasco sauce
2 dozen frankfurters

OUTDOORS   Melt butter in a saucepan on edge of grill. Add onion and cook until tender, but not brown. Stir in molasses, chili sauce, lemon juice, mustard, Worcestershire sauce, and Tabasco sauce. Bring to a boil. Reduce heat and simmer 10 minutes. Use to baste frankfurters during grilling.

INDOORS   Make barbecue sauce on range and cook frankfurters under broiler.
Makes 24 servings.

5 / Sizzling Lamb

When is a lamb chop not just a lamb chop? When it's marinated and grilled to perfection!

Lamb is the original choice for shish kebab; when cubed and skewered along with onions and tomatoes, it creates a gourmet offering. But did you know that you can barbecue legs of lamb and racks of lamb ribs to equal applause?

Here is a selection of superb lamb recipes, each with its own special spicing that will flavor lamb fit for a sheik or a caliph or a king. For lamb is both a staple and a specialty of many lands. So be a barbecue traveler. With these recipes as your passport, you can partake of such far-flung delights as lamb chops with pineapple from Hawaii, lamb risotto from New Zealand, or a leg of lamb with tomato sauce from Italy. Just a glance at the itinerary of recipes should convince you that the standard steak and hamburgers are by no means the only entree choices for your grill.

HAWAIIAN LUAU LAMB CHOPS

6	loin lamb chops, 1½ inches thick	2	tablespoons butter
½	teaspoon marjoram	1½	tablespoons grated orange rind
¾	teaspoon salt	½	cup orange juice
1	cup packaged bread stuffing	1½	teaspoons cornstarch
1	(9-ounce) can crushed pineapple	1	stick cinnamon, 1½ inches long
¼	cup golden raisins	¼	cup water
¼	teaspoon dry mustard	¼	cup curaçao or orange juice
¾	teaspoon ginger		

OUTDOORS Cut a pocket into the side of each lamb chop. Sprinkle chops with marjoram and ½ teaspoon of the salt. Combine bread stuffing, undrained pineapple, raisins, mustard, and ½ teaspoon of the ginger. Mix well and stuff each chop lightly; wrap any remaining dressing in foil to bake along with chops. Brown chops well on both sides in butter in skillet. Stir in orange rind and juice; cover. Place skillet on hot grill and cook until meat is fork tender (about 1 hour). In saucepan, mix together cornstarch, remaining ¼ teaspoon salt and ¼ teaspoon ginger, cinnamon, and water. Drain liquid from lamb chops and stir into cornstarch mixture; cook and stir over low heat until thickened and clear. Add curaçao and pour over chops. Garnish with orange slices, if desired.

INDOORS Stuff chops and brown in oven-proof skillet on range. Stir in orange rind and juice; cover. Place skillet in a 350-degree oven for about 1 hour, then proceed as above. *Makes 6 servings.*

Hawaiian Luau Lamb Chops

These lamb chops Hawaiian-style feature a pineapple stuffing and a delightful orange-flavored sauce. Easily adaptable to indoor or outdoor cooking, the chops are served here with a garnish of parsley and scalloped orange slices. Courtesy of American Lamb Council

LAMB CHOPS WITH SPICED TOMATO MARINADE

8 shoulder lamb chops
1 cup tomato puree
2 tablespoons chopped onion
1 tablespoon prepared horseradish
1 tablespoon Worcestershire sauce
1/4 cup wine vinegar
1/2 teaspoon salt
1 1/2 teaspoons sugar
1/8 teaspoon pepper

OUTDOORS   Arrange lamb chops in a flat pan. Combine tomato puree, onion, horseradish, Worcestershire sauce, and vinegar. Add salt, sugar, and pepper. Pour over lamb chops and marinate for one hour. Remove lamb chops from marinade and arrange on grill. Grill on first side for 5 minutes, basting occasionally with marinade mixture; then turn and grill for 5 minutes more or until done to your taste, continuing to baste.

INDOORS   After marinating chops as above, pour remaining marinade into small pan. Slide lamb chops under broiler. Turn after 5 minutes, baste with marinade, and broil for 5 minutes more, or until done.
Makes 8 servings.

SHERRY HERBED LAMB SHOULDER CHOPS

1 1/2 teaspoons salt
1/2 teaspoon pepper
1/2 teaspoon garlic powder
1 tablespoon dehydrated parsley flakes
2 tablespoons vinegar
6 shoulder lamb chops, about 1 inch thick
2 eggs, slightly beaten
1 cup fine dry bread crumbs
1/4 cup butter or margarine
1 (1-pound) can tomatoes
6 small white onions
1 cup sherry
1 teaspoon marjoram
2 tablespoons water
2 tablespoons flour

OUTDOORS Mix together salt, pepper, garlic powder, parsley flakes, and vinegar; rub mixture into lamb chops. Dip chops first into egg, then into bread crumbs, coating thoroughly. Melt butter in skillet on edge of grill and sauté chops until browned on both sides. In shallow baking pan mix together tomatoes, onions, sherry, and marjoram; add chops and place over hot grill for 30 minutes. Remove pan from grill and drain off ½ cup sauce; blend water with flour, then with the sauce until smooth. Stir mixture into remaining sauce around lamb; cook 30 minutes longer until lamb is tender.

INDOORS Sauté chops on range. Continue as above, cooking chops in a 325-degree oven for 30 minutes.
Makes 6 servings.

BARBECUED LAMB RIBLETS

4 pounds lamb ribs or breast
1 (8-ounce) can tomato sauce with mushrooms
3 tablespoons soy sauce
2 tablespoons brown sugar

½ teaspoon ginger
¼ teaspoon pepper
1 clove garlic, crushed
¼ cup white wine (optional)

OUTDOORS Cook ribs slowly about 5 inches above glowing coals, turning frequently, for about 1 hour. During last ½ hour of cooking, baste with barbecue sauce made by combining tomato sauce with soy sauce, sugar, ginger, pepper, garlic, and wine.

INDOORS Trim excess fat from ribs; place in flat pan. Bake in a 350-degree oven for 1 hour. Drain off fat. Proceed as above.
Makes 4 servings.

NEW ZEALAND LAMB RISOTTO

2 tablespoons oil	1 (10½-ounce) can
1 onion, sliced thin	condensed chicken
1 green pepper, slivered	consommé
1 cup long-grain rice	½ teaspoon oregano
1 tomato, cut into 6	¾ teaspoon salt
wedges	⅜ teaspoon pepper
¾ cup water	4 lamb shoulder chops

OUTDOORS   Heat oil in pan on grill, or indoors on range, add onion and green pepper, and cook until tender. Add rice and stir until rice is coated and slightly golden. Add tomato, water, chicken consommé, oregano, ½ teaspoon salt, and ¼ teaspoon pepper. Bring quickly to a boil. Cover pan, reduce heat, simmer 14 minutes or until rice is done. Season lamb chops with ¼ teaspoon salt and ⅛ teaspoon pepper. Place chops on grill for 5 minutes on each side, or until done to your taste. Place chops over rice mixture to serve.

INDOORS   Cook rice on range and chops under broiler.
Makes 4 servings.

SHISH KEBAB

4 pounds boned leg of lamb, cut in 1½-inch cubes	12 small onions, peeled
	¼ cup lemon juice
	¾ cup olive oil
4 medium green peppers, cut in 1½-inch squares	1 clove garlic, crushed
	½ teaspoon salt
12 cherry tomatoes	½ teaspoon dry mustard

OUTDOORS   On 12 long skewers, arrange alternating cubes of lamb and green pepper. Place a cherry tomato and an onion on the end of each. In a flat pan, combine lemon juice, olive oil, garlic, salt, and mustard. Place skewers side by side in the marinade, turning frequently for several hours before grilling. To cook, remove skewers from marinade and grill about 6 inches above hot coals, basting frequently with the remaining marinade. Grill, turning frequently, for about 15 minutes, depending on the degree of doneness desired.

INDOORS   Put skewers under broiler and cook 5 minutes per side.
Makes 8–12 servings.

ISLAND PINEAPPLE LAMB KABOBS

4 pounds boned leg of lamb	1 tablespoon prepared mustard
1 (20-ounce) can pineapple slices	2 teaspoons seasoned salt
¼ cup lemon juice	½ teaspoon oregano
¼ cup wine vinegar	2 sprigs mint
¼ cup catsup	2 cloves garlic, cut
½ cup sauterne wine	12 small white onions, parboiled or canned
3 tablespoons cooking oil	12 small plum tomatoes

OUTDOORS   Trim fat from lamb; cut meat into 1½-inch chunks. Combine 1 cup syrup drained from pineapple with lemon juice, vinegar, catsup, wine, oil, mustard, salt, and oregano. Add mint sprigs and cut garlic cloves. Combine with lamb and pineapple slices. Cover and refrigerate several hours or overnight. When ready to barbecue, discard mint and garlic. Thread 4 or 5 lamb chunks on each skewer. Grill over coals until meat is crusty and brown on outside and faintly pink inside. Brush frequently with marinade and turn often for even cooking. Thread onions and tomatoes on separate skewers. Grill, brushing with marinade, until heated and tinged with brown. Grill pineapple slices.

INDOORS   Cook kabobs under broiler, as above.
Makes 8–12 servings.

LAMB KABOBS WITH
SWEET-SOUR APPLE MARINADE

2 cups canned apple
sauce
¼ cup chili sauce
2 tablespoons vinegar
½ cup Italian-style salad
dressing
1 clove garlic, minced
1 teaspoon salt
½ teaspoon dry mustard

¼ teaspoon pepper
2½ pounds boned leg of
lamb
12 large mushrooms
2 green peppers, cut in
squares
12 small white onions,
parboiled

OUTDOORS Combine apple sauce, chili sauce, vinegar, salad
dressing, garlic, salt, mustard, and pepper. Cut lamb into
1½-inch chunks; trim most of fat and any gristle. Put lamb
in a bowl and pour apple sauce mixture over; let stand in
refrigerator overnight. To prepare skewers, remove lamb
chunks from marinade and drain well. Reserve marinade for
basting. Alternate lamb chunks, mushrooms, green peppers,
and onions on 6 9-inch skewers. Brush with marinade and
broil over open coals to desired doneness. Turn frequently
to cook evenly, brushing often with marinade. Serve sizzling
hot.

INDOORS Cook kabobs in preheated broiler.
Makes 4–6 servings.

BARBECUED LEG OF LAMB, ITALIAN STYLE

¼ cup salad oil
3 tablespoons wine
vinegar
2 tablespoons chopped
canned green chilies
3 cloves garlic, crushed
2½ teaspoons salt
1 teaspoon oregano

½ teaspoon mild dry
mustard
1 leg of lamb, about
4–5 pounds
1 (8-ounce) can tomato
sauce
2 tablespoons dark
brown sugar

OUTDOORS Combine oil, vinegar, chilies, and other seasonings; pour over lamb in shallow dish. Cover and marinate overnight, turning lamb once. Skewer lamb with rotisserie spit; reserve marinade. Place spit about 8 inches above hot grill. Roast 30 minutes per pound or until meat thermometer registers 175 degrees for medium doneness. Blend marinade, tomato sauce, and sugar in saucepan; brush some on lamb for last ½ hour roasting time. Heat remainder and serve with roast.

INDOORS Cook on indoor rotisserie spit, or roast in 350-degree oven for 30 minutes per pound, brushing with marinade the last half hour of cooking time as above.
Makes 6–8 servings.

TOMATO BARBECUE LAMB SPARERIBS

4 pounds lamb spareribs	1 tablespoon
1 medium onion, finely	Worcestershire sauce
chopped	¼ cup brown sugar
1 clove garlic, minced	¼ cup wine vinegar
1 teaspoon salt	1 (6-ounce) can tomato
⅛ teaspoon pepper	paste
½ teaspoon dry mustard	1 (1-pound) can tomato
	puree

OUTDOORS On grill or indoors on range, simmer spareribs in boiling water for 1 hour. Remove from heat and drain. Meanwhile, combine remaining ingredients in saucepan and bring to boil over medium heat. Simmer covered for 20 minutes. Place spareribs on grill for 8 minutes per side or to desired degree of doneness. Brush several times with barbecue sauce. Heat any remaining sauce and serve with spareribs.

INDOORS After simmering spareribs, place them under broiler and continue as above.
Makes 4 servings.

Tomato Barbecue Lamb Spareribs

A zesty barbecue sauce enhances the flavor of these lamb spareribs. Simmer ribs for 20 minutes, then grill, brushing with the sauce, and you'll have a delicious entree to present to family and friends. Served here with a macaroni salad. Courtesy of American Lamb Council

6 / Grilled Veal

Interested in a low-fat-content meat with a high degree of flavor? Veal is your answer.

Veal is young beef, aged from four weeks to one year. The most popular cuts have very white fat around the edges, but the meat itself has very little marbling or none at all. Select veal that is pale pink-white in color; avoid it when it is dull gray or red. The redder the veal, the older—and tougher—it is.

Tender young veal is the prime ingredient of every recipe in this chapter, which is designed to give you a full repertoire of veal know-how. The delicate flavor of veal needs careful seasoning, added to enhance the meat's taste rather than to overpower it. It's a light touch that produces the choicest morsels!

BARBECUED BREAST OF VEAL

6 pounds breast of veal	1/3 cup vinegar
1 teaspoon salt	2 tablespoons soy sauce
1/4 teaspoon pepper	1/2 cup orange juice
1/4 teaspoon paprika	1 tablespoon prepared
1/3 cup brown sugar	mustard

OUTDOORS   Season breast of veal with salt and pepper, rubbing well. Sprinkle paprika over top. Place on grill and brown quickly on each side. Stir sugar, vinegar, and soy sauce into orange juice. Add mustard. Brush veal with this marinade and turn frequently as veal is cooking. To serve, cut breast of veal into serving pieces of several ribs each.

INDOORS   Place seasoned veal in a pan and roast in a 350-degree oven, basting frequently with marinade. Cook about 2 hours or until fork tender.
Makes 6–8 servings.

ORANGE GLAZED VEAL ROAST

1/2 cup orange marmalade	2 tablespoons lemon juice
1 tablespoon prepared mustard	1 shoulder of veal roast, boned and rolled, about
1/2 teaspoon ginger	5 pounds

OUTDOORS   Combine orange marmalade, mustard, ginger, and lemon juice in a saucepan; simmer until marmalade is melted and mixture is hot. Place roast on a double thickness of heavy-duty aluminum foil large enough to wrap completely around roast. Turn up foil around meat and pour sauce over veal roast, turning roast so that all sides are coated with sauce. Seal foil tightly. Place on a hot grill; cook for about 15 minutes per pound of meat, rolling occasionally to turn the roast and redistribute marinade. Remove meat from foil and brown quickly if desired.

INDOORS   Place roast in foil in a pan; cook in a 350-degree oven for 15 minutes per pound, turning occasionally to distribute marinade. Open foil during the last 30 minutes of cooking so roast will brown.
Makes 8–10 servings.

ROTISSERIE SHOULDER OF VEAL

1 boned, rolled shoulder of veal roast, about 5 pounds
½ cup chili sauce
½ cup brown sugar
¼ cup prepared mustard
1 teaspoon Worcestershire sauce
½ teaspoon salt
¼ teaspoon pepper
¼ teaspoon garlic salt
¼ cup water

OUTDOORS   Place veal roast in a deep bowl. Combine remaining ingredients in a saucepan and bring to a boil; simmer for five minutes. Pour this marinade over veal and refrigerate for several hours, turning occasionally. Then remove veal from marinade, reserving the marinade for basting, and skewer veal roast securely on a revolving spit. (If desired, place veal roast directly on the grill instead.) Cook for about 15 minutes to the pound, basting often with marinade.

INDOORS   Cook veal roast in a pan in a 350-degree oven, 15 minutes per pound, basting as above.
Makes 8–10 servings.

GRILLED VEAL CORDON BLEU

12 thin slices veal, pounded flat	1 egg
½ teaspoon salt	½ teaspoon prepared mustard
¼ teaspoon pepper	1 cup bread crumbs
½ teaspoon oregano	1 tablespoon grated Parmesan cheese
6 thin slices ham	
6 slices Swiss cheese	¼ cup olive oil

OUTDOORS   Sprinkle veal slices with salt, pepper, and oregano. Top 6 slices of veal with a slice of ham and a slice of cheese; cover each with a slice of veal. Beat egg; add mustard. Combine bread crumbs and Parmesan cheese. Press edges around veal to seal tightly; dip each veal sandwich in beaten egg mixture, then in bread crumb mixture. Heat oil in a large skillet on the grill; brown each veal sandwich on both sides, then cover and cook for 15 minutes or until veal is tender.

INDOORS   Cook in skillet on the range.
Makes 6 servings.

GRILLED VEAL ALOHA

2 pounds thinly sliced veal cutlets	½ pound mushroom caps, sliced thin
1 (1-pound) can pineapple slices	2 tablespoons chopped parsley
½ teaspoon salt	¼ cup butter (for indoor cooking)
¼ teaspoon pepper	

OUTDOORS Arrange veal in a single layer in a large flat pan; pour juice drained from pineapple slices over veal. Sprinkle with salt and pepper. Let this marinate in refrigerator for several hours until ready to grill. Place each veal slice on a double-thick square of aluminum foil large enough to cover the meat; top with a pineapple slice, mushrooms, and parsley. Close aluminum packets over veal, folding edges tightly to seal, and place on a hot grill for 25 minutes.

INDOORS Melt butter in a heavy skillet; arrange marinated veal in skillet, top with pineapple, mushrooms, and parsley. Cover and simmer over low heat for 25 minutes.
Makes 6 servings.

STUFFED VEAL RIB CHOPS

½ pound mushrooms, sliced thin	10 pitted black olives, chopped
1 onion, diced	½ teaspoon salt
1 green pepper, diced	½ teaspoon thyme
2 tablespoons olive oil	8 veal rib chops
1 tomato, chopped	¼ cup olive oil (for indoor cooking)

OUTDOORS Sauté mushrooms, onion, and green pepper in olive oil until onion is translucent. Add chopped tomato, black olives, salt, and thyme for a minute more. Remove mixture with a slotted spoon. Cut a pocket in the side of each rib chop. Fill each pocket with a portion of the mixture and fasten closed with a toothpick. Place chops on a hot grill and brown on both sides; turn frequently for about 20 minutes or until tender.

INDOORS Add ¼ cup more olive oil to same skillet used for the filling and brown chops. Cover and simmer for 20 minutes or until tender.
Makes 8 servings.

VEAL CHOPS MARSALA

6 large veal rib chops
¼ cup melted butter
2 tablespoons parsley

½ teaspoon salt
¼ teaspoon pepper
½ cup Marsala wine

OUTDOORS Brush veal chops with melted butter mixed with parsley, salt, and pepper. Brown quickly on a hot grill or in a skillet on grill. Brush with wine and turn frequently on the grill until chops are tender, about 20 minutes; if you are using a skillet, simply pour the wine over the chops and simmer until tender.

INDOORS Cook in skillet on the range.
Makes 6 servings.

VEAL ROLLS

2 pounds thin slices veal, pounded flat
½ teaspoon salt
¼ teaspoon pepper
2 cups prepared seasoned poultry stuffing

1 pound thinly sliced boiled ham
½ cup sauterne wine
½ cup beef bouillon
1 tablespoon lemon juice
1 teaspoon sugar

OUTDOORS Sprinkle veal slices with salt and pepper. Prepare poultry stuffing according to directions on the package, making a moist stuffing. Spread stuffing on the top surface of each slice of veal; top with a thin slice of ham. Roll up each slice of veal carefully, jelly-roll fashion, starting at a short side. Tie with white string in several places. Combine wine, bouillon, lemon juice, and sugar in a saucepan; simmer for several minutes. Roll each veal roll in this sauce and then place on the grill, basting frequently with the sauce and turning rolls frequently during 20-25 minutes of cooking time.

INDOORS Arrange veal rolls in a large skillet and pour sauce over all. Simmer for 20 minutes or until tender.
Makes 6–8 servings.

VEAL KABOBS

2 pounds cubed veal
2 large green peppers, cut in squares
1 (1-pound) can pineapple chunks, drained

12 mushroom caps
½ teaspoon onion salt
½ teaspoon salt
¼ teaspoon pepper
¼ cup butter, melted

OUTDOORS Skewer veal, green peppers, pineapple chunks, and mushroom caps on 6 individual skewers. Stir onion salt, salt, and pepper into melted butter. Brush kabobs liberally with this mixture. Cook over medium-hot coals for about 12 minutes, brushing several times with the remaining butter mixture. Turn frequently.

INDOORS Cook under broiler.
Makes 6 servings.

VEAL-BEEF SKILLET DINNER

1 pound ground beef
½ pound ground veal
1 envelope onion gravy mix
1¼ cups cold water
½ cup cold milk

½ teaspoon salt
1⅓ cups mashed potato flakes
1 (1-pound) can peas and carrots, drained
2 tablespoons butter

OUTDOORS In a medium-size skillet, combine ground meats and contents of gravy mix envelope. Pat the meat along the

Veal-Beef Skillet Dinner

Try this unusual pie of peas and carrots with a beef and veal crust and a mashed potato topping. It's a one-dish meal that will satisfy the heartiest appetite. Courtesy of R. T. French Company

bottom and sides of the skillet. Cook over low heat on the grill until meat is done. Drain off excess fat. Meanwhile, make mashed potatoes by combining water, milk, and salt, adding potato flakes, and stirring with a fork. When meat is done, spoon peas and carrots into the center of the meat crust. Spread prepared mashed potatoes over the top. Dot with butter. Cover and return to heat until vegetables and potatoes are hot, about 15–20 minutes. Serve in wedges.

INDOORS Cook in skillet on the range.
Makes 4–6 servings.

SKILLET VEAL AND PEPPERS

¼ cup olive oil
1 clove garlic, minced
2 pounds cubed veal
2 onions, sliced thin
4 green peppers, sweet
   Italian variety, cut in
   squares

1 (1-pound) can whole
   tomatoes
1 (6-ounce) can tomato
   paste
½ teaspoon oregano
½ teaspoon salt
¼ teaspoon pepper

OUTDOORS   Heat oil in a skillet on grill; brown minced garlic.
Add cubes of veal and brown on all sides; push aside and
sauté sliced onion and peppers until limp. Add tomatoes and
tomato paste. Add oregano, salt, and pepper. Stir all together
and simmer, covered, for 30 minutes.

INDOORS   Cook in skillet on the range.
Makes 6–8 servings.

7/Blazed Pork

The mere mention of a barbecue seems to conjure up visions of succulent spareribs dripping with mouth-watering sauce, and here you will find sparerib tricks to make these visions a reality!

Other cuts of pork, including pork chops, ham steaks, and sausages, are convenient to grill over the open fire. A variety of fruits are often used in pork recipes to enhance the flavor of the meat, and to add a hint of sweetness to your barbecue.

Young pork is grayish-pink in color; older meat is light rose. High-quality pork is well marbled with firm, white fat and its bones are porous and pinkish in color. Always cook pork to the well-done stage.

Try any of the recipes included at your next barbecue— your guests are sure to be delighted with the piquant taste of pork cooked over the glowing coals!

BARBECUED SPARERIBS WITH FRUIT

6 pounds (2 racks) pork spareribs	2 tablespoons soy sauce
1½ teaspoons salt	1 tablespoon celery seed
1 lemon, sliced thin	2 tablespoons Worcestershire sauce
⅓ cup unsulphured molasses	Green-tipped bananas, cut in chunks
⅓ cup prepared mustard	Pineapple chunks
⅓ cup vinegar	Maraschino cherries

OUTDOORS   Cut spareribs into serving pieces; place them, meaty side up, in a shallow, foil-lined baking pan. Sprinkle with salt. Top with lemon slices. Bake in a moderate oven (350 degrees) for 1 hour. Remove from oven; pour off fat. Refrigerate. When ready to grill, combine remaining ingredients, except for fruit, to make sauce. Place spareribs on grill 6–8 inches from heat; brush with sauce after 15 minutes. Cook 15 minutes longer, brushing frequently with sauce. Alternate banana and pineapple chunks and cherries on skewers. Brush with barbecue sauce and grill last 10 minutes of cooking time, until fruit is heated.

INDOORS   (Omit refrigeration unless preparing for later cooking.) Bake in a 350-degree oven for 1 hour. Pour off fat. Brush

with sauce as above. Return to oven, basting frequently with sauce. Add fruit to pan after 20 minutes; baste with sauce and cook 10–15 minutes longer.
Makes 8 servings.

APPLE 'N SPICE SPARERIBS

    4 pounds pork spareribs
1½ teaspoons salt
    2 cups apple sauce

⅓ cup light corn syrup
¼ teaspoon ground cloves
¼ teaspoon paprika

OUTDOORS Using kitchen shears, snip meat, ½ inch down between tops of rib bones. Fold meat under. Place spareribs, underside up, on the grill and sprinkle with salt. Grill for 15 minutes, turning often. Combine apple sauce, syrup, and cloves; spoon over meat. Sprinkle with paprika. Continue cooking on grill for 30 minutes longer or until ribs are tender. To serve, cut into serving pieces with kitchen shears.

INDOORS Prepare spareribs as above. Cook under broiler for 15 minutes. Spoon on sauce, add paprika, and continue to cook in a 350-degree oven for 30 minutes, or until tender.
Makes 6 servings.

POLYNESIAN RIBS

Uses Pork Chops

    3 pounds pork spareribs,
      cut into serving portions
    1 tablespoon garlic salt
    1 (8-ounce) can tomato
      sauce
  ½ cup apricot preserves
    1 teaspoon soy sauce
    1 teaspoon sugar

1 teaspoon minced onion
1 teaspoon prepared
  mustard
½ teaspoon salt
¼ teaspoon monosodium
  glutamate
⅛ teaspoon ginger

Polynesian Ribs

A sauce that combines the spiciness of tomatoes with the sweetness of apricots is the secret to success here. Baste the ribs with the sauce while they cook, and they will absorb its delightful flavor. Serve with a tossed salad, corn-on-the cob, and thick slices of bread. Courtesy of Hunt-Wesson Company

OUTDOORS Rub ribs with garlic salt; cook 4 inches above hot coals, turning occasionally, for about 1 hour or until done. Meanwhile, combine tomato sauce, apricot preserves, soy sauce, sugar, onion, mustard, salt, monosodium glutamate, and ginger in a saucepan; simmer 10 minutes. Baste ribs often with sauce during the last 15 minutes of cooking.

INDOORS Place ribs in a flat pan and bake in a 350-degree oven. Proceed as above.
Makes 4 servings.

CURRIED APPLE PORK CHOPS

2 cups apple sauce
½ cup apple juice
⅓ cup raisins
⅓ cup finely chopped onion
1 teaspoon grated lemon rind

1 teaspoon curry powder
½ teaspoon ginger
½ teaspoon salt
½ cup brown sugar
6 pork chops, cut ¾ inch thick

OUTDOORS Combine all ingredients except pork chops. Brown chops on both sides on grill, then place in a foil pan. (To make foil pan, use a 2-foot length of 18-inch-wide heavy-duty aluminum foil; fold in half lengthwise and turn up edges 2 inches all around. Fold corners closed.) Pour curried apple sauce over chops, cover pan with additional foil, and cook about 45 minutes. Remove foil cover and cook for 15 minutes more or until fork tender. To serve, spoon sauce left in pan over chops.

INDOORS Brown chops under broiler and proceed as above, using an aluminum pan in a 350-degree oven.
Makes 6 servings.

PORK CHOPS CHILI

6 double-thickness pork
chops (have butcher
slit pocket in each)
1 (15½-ounce) can
barbecue beans

½ cup chili sauce
½ teaspoon salt
⅛ teaspoon pepper

OUTDOORS Spoon barbecue beans into pocket of each pork chop. Close pockets with toothpicks. Spread chili sauce over both sides of chops and sprinkle with salt and pepper. Grill until thoroughly cooked.

INDOORS Cook chops in pan under broiler, turning once, about 20 minutes on each side.
Makes 6 servings.

PORK CHOPS WITH ORIENTAL SAUCE

½ cup frozen orange juice
concentrate, undiluted
⅔ cup pineapple juice
3 tablespoons lemon juice
¼ cup honey

1 tablespoon
Worcestershire sauce
2 tablespoons soy sauce
1 tablespoon dry mustard
2 cloves garlic, mashed
8 pork chops

OUTDOORS Thoroughly combine all ingredients except pork chops; whip vigorously with a wire whisk. Arrange pork chops in a flat pan and pour sauce over all. Cover and marinate in refrigerator for 24 hours. Brown pork chops on both sides on a hot grill. Place pork chops in a foil pan (see Curried Apple Pork Chops, p. 71, for directions to make foil pan). Pour remaining marinade over chops, cover pan with additional aluminum foil, and cook about 45 minutes. Remove cover and cook for 15 minutes more or until fork tender. To serve, spoon sauce left in pan over chops.

INDOORS Brown marinated pork chops under broiler. Continue cooking as above, using an aluminum pan in a 350-degree oven.
Makes 8 servings.

PEANUT PORK LOIN

1 pork loin roast, about 4 pounds
½ teaspoon salt
¼ teaspoon pepper

¼ cup smooth-style peanut butter
½ cup orange juice

OUTDOORS Sprinkle pork loin with salt and pepper. Combine peanut butter and orange juice into smooth sauce, using a wire whisk if necessary. Insert spit of rotisserie through roast, balancing it carefully. Brush roast with peanut-orange mixture and cook for about 2½ hours, basting frequently with remaining sauce.

INDOORS Use a rotisserie unit or cook in roasting pan in a 350-degree oven.
Makes 6–8 servings.

KIELBASI AND KIDNEY BEANS

2 Polish sausages (Kielbasi), about 6 inches long
½ cup chopped onions
2 tablespoons butter
½ cup long-grain white rice

1 (10½-ounce) can beef bouillon
2 (1-pound) cans red kidney beans
2 tablespoons chili sauce
¼ teaspoon salt

OUTDOORS Cut half of one sausage in ¼-inch slices. Sauté with onion in butter in a skillet, until onion is transparent. Add rice and bouillon. Bring to boil, cover and cook until rice is done. Drain and rinse kidney beans, and stir in chili sauce, and salt. Slice remaining whole sausage in half crosswise, then slice all 3 halves lengthwise. Place on top of kidney bean mixture like spokes of a wheel. Cover and cook over fire until bubbly.

INDOORS Cook in skillet on the range.
Makes 6–8 servings.

SAUSAGE KABOBS

2 (1-pound) packages brown-and-serve sausage links	½ cup chopped onion
	2 tablespoons oil
2 apples, quartered	⅛ teaspoon basil
1 large green pepper, cut into 1-inch pieces	¼ teaspoon garlic salt
	⅛ teaspoon pepper
6 small canned or boiled potatoes, peeled and cut in half	½ cup water
	1 (8-ounce) can tomato sauce with mushrooms
	¼ cup brown sugar

OUTDOORS Alternate sausage links, apples, green pepper, and potatoes on 6 skewers, beginning and ending with sausage. Place rack over hot coals and grill about 10 minutes on each side, until sausage browns. Baste with sauce made by browning onion in oil until tender, then adding basil, garlic salt, pepper, water, tomato sauce, and sugar, and simmering about 15 minutes.

INDOORS Place kabobs on a broiler rack and broil 6 minutes on each side, basting as above.
Makes 6 servings.

Sausage Kabobs

For imaginative kabobs, alternate sausages with slices of apple, green pepper, and potato on skewers, and baste with a simple barbecue sauce. Serve with remaining sauce and a loaf of Hot Buttered Garlic Bread. Courtesy of Hunt-Wesson Company

SAUSAGES AND BAKED BEANS

8 country link pork
    sausages

2 (1-pound) cans baked
    beans
4 spiced apple ring slices

OUTDOORS Fry sausages in 2-quart saucepan until nicely browned. Remove to paper towel, drain. Pour off excess fat, add beans to saucepan; top with apple slices and sausages. Cook over fire until mixture is bubbly.

INDOORS   Cook in saucepan on the range.
Makes 4 servings.

GRILLED HAM WITH RAISIN-CURRANT SAUCE

2 ham steaks, about 1 pound each	¾ cup pineapple juice
½ cup seedless raisins	1 tablespoon cornstarch
½ cup currant jelly	½ teaspoon dry mustard

OUTDOORS   With a sharp knife, slash fat edges of ham steaks to prevent curling. Combine raisins, jelly, pineapple juice, cornstarch, and dry mustard in a saucepan; cook, stirring over low heat, until sauce is clear and thickened. Place saucepan on the edge of the grill to keep warm during time ham is cooking. Place ham steaks over hot coals; cook for 5 minutes on each side. Serve with hot Raisin-Currant Sauce.

INDOORS   Keep sauce warm on range while cooking ham under broiler.
Makes 4–6 servings.

HAM STICKS HAWAIIAN

1 (3-pound) oblong canned ham	2 tablespoons sugar
1 (9-ounce) can crushed pineapple	1 tablespoon vinegar
	2 teaspoons cornstarch
½ cup firmly packed brown sugar	⅛ teaspoon cinnamon
	⅛ teaspoon ground cloves
	16 long buns

OUTDOORS   Remove ham from can and slice lengthwise into four equal portions, then cut each slice lengthwise into four sticks. Dip 2 tablespoons juice out of crushed pineapple and make glaze by combining juice with brown sugar. Spread glaze over ham sticks and grill until hot. Meanwhile, make a Hawaiian sauce by combining pineapple with sugar, vinegar, cornstarch, cinnamon, and cloves; cook on edge of grill until clear and thick, stirring occasionally. Place each glazed ham stick on a heated bun and pass the Hawaiian sauce.

INDOORS   Cook ham sticks under broiler, sauce on range. *Makes 16 servings.*

POLYNESIAN PINEAPPLE 'N HAM

1 center-cut ham slice, 1½ inches thick	1 tablespoon dry mustard
1 (20-ounce) can pineapple slices	½ teaspoon ginger
⅓ cup rum, or ¼ cup orange juice	2 tablespoons brown sugar
	1 tablespoon butter
	2 (1-pound) cans yams

OUTDOORS   Trim fat from ham. Brown ham lightly on both sides on grill over hot coals. Drain pineapple, reserving ½ cup syrup. Blend the ½ cup pineapple syrup with rum, mustard, ginger, sugar, and butter and heat in small pan. Place ham slice in center of large piece of heavy-duty aluminum foil. (Foil should be large enough to enclose ham, pineapple, and yams with a little free space for steam to gather.) Fold up edges of foil and pour in warm rum syrup. Double-fold edges of foil securely. Grill about 8 inches above coals, turning every 15 minutes, for 45 minutes. Open packet; arrange drained pineapple slices and yams around and over ham. Spoon sauce over all to moisten. Close foil loosely and continue grilling 10 minutes longer; open packet and grill another 5 minutes until heated through.

INDOORS   Brown ham under broiler. Proceed as above, cooking ham packet in a 350-degree oven.
Makes 6 servings.

Polynesian Pineapple 'n Ham

Cook ham, pineapple, and yams in a foil packet while they soak up a warm rum syrup. The result is a remarkable taste treat—without any baking pans to scrub! Courtesy of Pineapple Growers Association

SHOTGUN STEW

1 (10-ounce) package
    baby lima beans frozen
    in butter sauce, in
    cooking pouch
1 (10-ounce) package
    whole kernel corn
    frozen in butter sauce,
    in cooking pouch
1 (7-ounce) package
    spaghetti, uncooked
2 tablespoons salt

1 pound cooked ham,
    cut in ½-inch cubes
1 pound bacon, diced
1 (4½-ounce) jar sliced
    mushrooms, drained
2 (28-ounce) cans stewed
    tomatoes
¼ teaspoon seasoned
    pepper
¼ teaspoon celery seed
¼ teaspoon onion salt

OUTDOORS Slip pouches of lima beans and corn into boiling water. Bring water to second boil; continue cooking 14 minutes. Do not cover pan. Place spaghetti in boiling water to which 2 tablespoons of salt have been added; cook until nearly tender, then drain and rinse. Sauté ham and bacon in large Dutch oven until slightly browned. Drain excess drippings and move meat to one side; sauté mushrooms in remaining fat. Add all ingredients to the meat mixture. Stir gently until blended; simmer 30 minutes on the grill.

INDOORS Prepare stew as above. Simmer on range for 30 minutes.
Makes 8–12 servings.

NORTH WOODS BREAKFAST

1 (1-pound) package
    bacon, sliced

1 (1-pound) can sliced
    potatoes, drained
4 eggs

OUTDOORS Cut bacon into 1-inch pieces. Cook in skillet on grill until crisp; remove and drain, reserving drippings. Cook potatoes in 2 tablespoons of drippings until lightly browned. Arrange bacon pieces around sides of skillet. In center, arrange potatoes in four nests and break an egg into each. Cover and cook until eggs are done to your taste.

INDOORS   Cook in skillet on the range.
Makes 4 servings.

8 / Kindled Poultry

Poultry is a "natural" for your grill! It can be cooked in so many ways and combined with so many exciting flavors that recipe variations seem endless. As a bonus, it is a low-calorie, high-protein-content food—a tasty treat for weight watchers.

One of the easiest and most flavorful recipes is foil-baked

chicken, which is grilled while it soaks up its own marinade. Even when wrapped in foil throughout the cooking period, it emerges browned, with a delicious sticky surface. Serve the chicken right in the foil and let each person unwrap his own savory packet.

Turkey, duck, and Cornish hen, as well as chicken, are easily adaptable to the rotisserie. Be sure to carefully balance the fowl on the spit so each will rotate smoothly and brown evenly. If you are cooking several chickens or hens at one time, tying one with its legs up and another with its legs down often does the trick. These acrobatics may seem excessive in theory, but, in practice, prove worth it, since rotisserie cooking results in a toothsome barbecue every time.

TEXAS-STYLE CHICKEN

2 (2-pound) broiler chickens, split
¼ cup oil
1 (8-ounce) can tomato sauce
½ cup water
1 tablespoon Worcestershire sauce
2 teaspoons prepared mustard
2 teaspoons sugar
½ teaspoon chili powder
1 clove garlic, crushed
1 small onion, finely chopped

OUTDOORS   Brush chicken with 2 tablespoons of the oil; place on grill about 5 inches above glowing coals. Cook 20 minutes, turning occasionally, until browned. Meanwhile, in a saucepan, combine remaining oil, tomato sauce, water, Worcestershire sauce, mustard, sugar, chili powder, garlic, and onion; bring to a boil and simmer 10 minutes. Baste chicken with sauce, turning frequently, until tender and cooked through (about 15 minutes longer).

INDOORS   After brushing chicken with oil, place in a pan and

cook under broiler; baste with sauce and continue as above.
Makes 4 servings.

✓ LEMONY BARBECUED CHICKEN

1 (6-ounce) can frozen lemonade, thawed, undiluted	¼ cup prepared yellow mustard
1 cup catsup	¼ cup butter
¾ cup water	2 tablespoons instant minced onion
¼ cup Worcestershire sauce	2 (3-pound) fryer chickens, cut in pieces

OUTDOORS Combine lemonade, catsup, and water. Add Worcestershire sauce, mustard, butter, and onion. Bring to a boil and simmer 5 minutes. Broil chicken on the grill, basting frequently with this sauce. Turn several times during cooking.

INDOORS Cook chicken under broiler about 20 minutes on each side.
Makes 8 servings.

✓ ROTISSERIE CHICKEN WITH ORANGE GLAZE

2 (3-pound) broiler chickens	2 tablespoons soy sauce
1 teaspoon monosodium glutamate	1 teaspoon instant minced onion
1 teaspoon salt	½ teaspoon celery seed
1 (6-ounce) can frozen orange juice concentrate, thawed, undiluted	¼ teaspoon ginger
	¼ teaspoon Tabasco sauce

OUTDOORS Sprinkle cavity of each chicken with monosodium glutamate and ½ teaspoon of the salt. Tie legs together, then tie to tail. Secure on revolving spit. Cook over grill for about 1 hour. Combine orange juice concentrate with soy sauce, minced onion, celery seed, ginger, Tabasco sauce, and remaining ½ teaspoon salt. Brush chickens with sauce. Cook chickens another 20 minutes, brushing frequently.

INDOORS   Use indoor rotisserie. To barbecue chicken in oven, place in shallow roasting pan; bake, uncovered, in 375-degree oven for 1 hour and 15 minutes. Brush with sauce and bake another 15 minutes, brushing frequently with sauce and the pan drippings.
Makes 6 servings.

SAVORY BARBECUED BROILERS

1 (1½-ounce) envelope seasoning mix for Sloppy Joes	4 tablespoons butter
	3 broiler chickens, about 2 pounds each, split
½ cup catsup	1 teaspoon salt
½ cup water	½ teaspoon pepper
3 tablespoons Worcestershire sauce	¼ cup salad oil

OUTDOORS   To make barbecue sauce, combine in a saucepan the seasoning mix, catsup, water, Worcestershire sauce, and butter. Bring mixture to a boil; reduce heat and cook 4 minutes, stirring occasionally. Sprinkle both sides of chicken with salt and pepper; brush with salad oil. Grill chicken over charcoal 40 minutes or until tender, turning often and basting continually with barbecue sauce.

INDOORS   Cook chicken under broiler, basting as above.
Makes 6 servings.

Savory Barbecued Broilers

Whether you're cooking for your family or entertaining on a large scale, barbecued chicken is an ideal entree. Add a new twist by making your own barbecue sauce from a popular seasoning mix. Broilers are served here with remaining sauce and potato salad. Courtesy of R. T. French Company

CHICKEN WITH ORANGE DUNKING SAUCE

3 broiler chickens, 3 pounds each, quartered

3 teaspoons monosodium glutamate

1 teaspoon salt

1/4 teaspoon pepper

1/4 cup salad oil

Orange Dunking Sauce:

1 cup orange marmalade
¼ cup sugar
¼ cup vinegar
2 tablespoons unsulphured molasses

1 tablespoon Worcestershire sauce
1 tablespoon curry powder
1 teaspoon salt
½ teaspoon ginger
1 teaspoon Tabasco sauce

OUTDOORS Sprinkle each chicken with monosodium glutamate, salt, and pepper. Place chicken, skin side up, on grill; brush with oil. Cook for about 1 hour; chicken is done when leg twists easily out of thigh joint and meat is fork tender. Meanwhile, combine remaining ingredients in a saucepan to make dunking sauce. Place on edge of grill; bring to a boil; simmer 5 minutes, stirring constantly until marmalade is melted and all ingredients are blended. Serve with chicken.

INDOORS Cook chicken under broiler. Cook sauce on range. *Makes 12 servings with 2 cups of sauce.*

CHICKEN CAPRICE

2 cups apple sauce
½ cup apple juice
2 tablespoons lemon juice
1 teaspoon grated lemon rind
½ cup brown sugar
½ teaspoon dry mustard

½ cup toasted slivered almonds
1 broiler chicken, cut in quarters
¼ cup butter, melted
½ teaspoon salt

OUTDOORS Combine apple sauce, apple juice, lemon juice, lemon rind, sugar, mustard, and almonds. Brush chicken with butter and season with salt on both sides. Brown chicken on both sides on grill, about 4 inches from heat. Place chicken in a flat pan and pour apple sauce mixture over chicken. Cover pan loosely with foil and place on grill. Cook for 45 minutes, turning chicken once and spooning sauce over it several times. Remove foil cover and cook for an additional 15 minutes. Serve hot with remaining sauce spooned over chicken.

INDOORS Use broiler to brown chicken. Proceed as above, cooking in a 350-degree oven.
Makes 4 servings.

CHICKEN WITH ZESTY SAUCE

¼ cup unsulphured molasses
¼ cup vinegar
1 (8-ounce) can tomato sauce
½ teaspoon dry mustard
½ teaspoon chili powder
⅛ teaspoon Tabasco sauce
3 broiler chickens about 2 pounds, split

OUTDOORS Combine molasses, vinegar, tomato sauce, mustard, chili powder, and Tabasco sauce in a saucepan; bring to a boil. Reduce heat and simmer 5 minutes. Arrange chickens, skin side up, on the grill; baste with sauce, turning several times during grilling. Cook for about 30–40 minutes.

INDOORS Cook chicken under broiler, basting as above.
Makes 6 servings.

BARBECUED CHICKEN LEGS

1 teaspoon dry mustard
1 teaspoon salt
⅛ teaspoon garlic salt
1 teaspoon paprika
⅓ cup vinegar
½ cup salad oil
½ teaspoon Tabasco sauce
1 tablespoon unsulphured molasses
12 broiler chicken legs

OUTDOORS Mix together mustard, salt, garlic salt, and paprika. Stir in vinegar, oil, Tabasco sauce, and molasses. Place chicken legs on grill, skin side up. Brush with barbecue sauce until tender, brushing frequently.

INDOORS Cook chicken under broiler, basting as above.
Makes 6 servings.

CHICKEN BREASTS PROVENÇAL

3 whole chicken breasts, cut in half
1 teaspoon monosodium glutamate
½ teaspoon salt
½ teaspoon paprika
½ cup butter
1 clove garlic
½ pound mushrooms
1 medium onion
1 green pepper, cut in strips
1 medium eggplant, cut in ½-inch slices
1 (1-pound) can tomatoes
1 (8-ounce) can tomato sauce
¼ teaspoon Tabasco sauce
¼ teaspoon dried leaf basil
¼ teaspoon dried leaf tarragon
2 tablespoons grated Parmesan cheese
2 tablespoons chopped parsley

OUTDOORS Sprinkle chicken with monosodium glutamate, salt, and paprika. Melt butter in a large skillet on grill. Add chicken breasts and brown on both sides. Remove chicken. Chop garlic, mushroom stems, and onion. Add to skillet with green pepper strips and eggplant. When eggplant slices are lightly browned, add tomatoes, tomato sauce, Tabasco sauce, basil, and tarragon. Return chicken to skillet; cover and simmer 45 minutes. Add mushroom caps; cook 5 minutes longer. To serve, sprinkle with Parmesan cheese and parsley.

INDOORS Cook in skillet on the range.
Makes 6 servings.

CHICKEN THIGHS WITH PINEAPPLE MARINADE

1 cup pineapple juice	2 tablespoons brown sugar
1/4 cup catsup	1 teaspoon dry mustard
1 tablespoon soy sauce	1/4 teaspoon cloves
2 tablespoons white vinegar	1/2 teaspoon monosodium glutamate
1 tablespoon Worcestershire sauce	1/4 teaspoon paprika
	12 chicken thighs

OUTDOORS Combine all ingredients except chicken thighs; whip vigorously. Place thighs in a large plastic bag set in a bowl; pour pineapple marinade into the bag. Close bag securely; refrigerate for several hours, turning bag occasionally to redistribute marinade. Remove thighs from marinade; place on a hot grill and cook for 20 minutes, turning occasionally and basting with the remaining marinade. When fork tender, serve. 8-77 USED Quarters chicken

INDOORS Bake in a 350-degree oven for 20 minutes, or until tender, basting occasionally.
Makes 6 servings.

FOIL-BAKED CHICKEN

2 broiler chickens, 3 pounds each, quartered	1 lemon
	1 bottle barbecue sauce

OUTDOORS Rub quarters of chicken with cut lemon. Arrange in a flat pan and pour barbecue sauce over chicken; place in refrigerator and allow to marinate for several hours, turning to redistribute marinade. Before cooking, place each well-coated quarter of chicken on a double-thick square of aluminum foil; fold and seal tightly. Place on a hot grill for 30–40 minutes, turning once. Serve in the foil packet.

INDOORS   Bake in a 375-degree oven for 30 minutes. Remove chicken from foil before serving.
Makes 8 servings.

ROTISSERIE DUCK WITH SHERRY-GINGER SAUCE

1 duck, about 4 pounds	1 tablespoon soy sauce
1 orange	1 tablespoon honey
2 tablespoons sherry	¼ teaspoon ginger

OUTDOORS   Wash and dry duck thoroughly. Cut orange in half; rub a cut side over the skin of the duck and over the cavity. Squeeze several tablespoons of juice and grate a table-spoon of orange rind from the orange half into a small bowl; then put remaining parts of orange inside the duck. Add the remaining ingredients to the rind and juice; stir well. Place duck on the rotisserie spit, tying securely. Cook for about 1½ hours, basting with the sherry-ginger sauce during the last 20 minutes of cooking. Drain duck, discarding orange. Skin should be crisp and highly glazed in appearance. Cut in quarters to serve.

INDOORS   Cook duck, breast side up, in a 375-degree oven.
Makes 4 servings.

ROTISSERIE SMOKED TURKEY

1 turkey, about 12 pounds	½ teaspoon garlic salt
1 tablespoon salt	½ teaspoon paprika
¼ pound butter	Hickory chips

OUTDOORS   Remove giblets and wash turkey. Rub salt over the inside cavity and the skin. Place turkey on the rotisserie spit, carefully balanced so it will turn evenly. Tie wings and legs securely. Melt butter in a saucepan; add garlic salt and paprika. Brush turkey with this butter mixture frequently while it rotates. Sprinkle hickory chips over hot coals several times during cooking. Roast for about 4 hours or until turkey is tender to the piercing of a fork in the densest portion. Remove from grill and let stand for 20 minutes to make carving easier.

INDOORS   Use a 300-degree oven for 4 hours.
Makes 8–10 servings.

✓ROTISSERIE CORNISH HENS

¼ cup finely chopped celery	¼ cup orange juice
1 large clove garlic, minced	2 tablespoons grated orange rind
2 tablespoons butter	4 Rock Cornish hens, about 1 pound each
1 (10¾-ounce) can condensed tomato soup	

OUTDOORS   In saucepan, cook celery with garlic in butter until tender. Add tomato soup, orange juice, and orange rind. Cook on edge of grill over low heat for 10 minutes, stirring occasionally. Truss hens on spit, close together. Balance; tie securely. Place over glowing coals. Place drip-pan under hens. Cook 30 minutes. Baste with sauce; cook 1 hour more or until tender, basting every 15 minutes.

INDOORS   Cook sauce on range. Place hens in roasting pan in a 350-degree oven for 45 minutes to 1 hour.
Makes 4 servings.

9/Fish on the Fire

A mess of fish on the fire has long been a natural sight for those who live by the shore and value a fast "catch 'em, clean 'em, cook 'em" routine. Now, with fish markets in most cities and with the availability of many varieties of frozen fish, even the landlocked barbecuer can cook up a tasty "catch."

When buying fish look for bright, clear, bulging eyes and

firm flesh. Avoid any fish with an unpleasant odor. Fresh fish is highly perishable, so wrap it tightly and keep it in the coldest part of the refrigerator until ready to use.

For whole fish, allow one pound per serving. For fillets and steaks, count on one-third to one-half pound for each person. Avoid overcooking fish and use foil as recommended to give even heat and prevent scorching of the delicate skin.

Here you will find a variety of recipes from every waterfront, each with a fish story of its own!

BROILED LOBSTER

4 live lobsters	¼ cup lemon juice
¼ cup butter, melted	

OUTDOORS   Split the lobsters just before you are ready to broil them (or, if you are squeamish, have them split at the market). Remove the intestinal vein and stomach of each lobster. Brush the meat with melted butter and lemon juice. Place lobsters flesh side down on the grill and cook for 2 minutes; then turn shell side down and cook for about 15 minutes or until lobster meat is opaque. Serve with additional melted butter mixed with lemon juice for dipping chunks of lobster as you eat.

INDOORS   Use the broiler.
Makes 4 servings.

GRILLED KING CRAB LEGS

¼ pound butter	2 (12-ounce) packages
2 tablespoons lemon juice	frozen precooked
¼ teaspoon salt	Alaskan king crab legs,
Dash of pepper	thawed

OUTDOORS In a small saucepan on the edge of the grill, combine butter, lemon juice, salt, and pepper; stir until completely melted and blended. Arrange king crab legs on grill and brush with melted butter sauce. Grill for about 5 minutes on each side, being careful not to overcook and toughen the crab meat. Baste frequently during grilling time. Remove king crab legs from grill and pour remaining butter sauce over. Serve at once.

INDOORS Make butter sauce in saucepan on range. Cook crab legs under broiler.
Makes 4 servings.

CLAM BAKE ON THE GRILL

3 dozen steamer clams in the shell, scrubbed
6 ears of corn in husks, soaked in salted water
6 small baking potatoes
6 frozen lobster tails, thawed
6 chicken-breast halves
6 whole onions
2 lemons, cut in wedges
½ pound butter, melted
Salt
Rockweed or seaweed, or a thick layer of cheesecloth soaked in salted water

OUTDOORS Prepare 6 18-inch squares of double-layered heavy-duty aluminum foil. Place an 8-inch square of foil in the center of each large foil square and top with a thick layer of rockweed. Place 6 clams on each square on the rockweed; arrange corn (silk removed but husks intact), potatoes, lobster tails, chicken, and onions atop the clams, making six equal packets. Turn up edges of foil. Top with a layer of rockweed and pour a glass of water into each packet just before final sealing. Turn sealed side of each aluminum foil packet down on an additional 18-inch square of foil and seal securely.

Place the six packets on a hot grill for 30 minutes, turn and cook for 20–30 minutes longer. Serve in the packet with lemon wedges and melted butter.

INDOORS   Make packets, as above. Bake in a 350-degree oven for 1 hour.
Makes 6 servings.

SHRIMPBURGERS

1 (12-ounce) package frozen, shelled and deveined cooked shrimp
3 tablespoons butter
3 tablespoons flour
¾ cup milk
1 cup cooked rice
½ cup grated American cheese

2 tablespoons grated onion
1 teaspoon salt
⅛ teaspoon pepper
Dash of cayenne
½ teaspoon curry powder
1 cup fine dry bread crumbs
6 hamburger buns

OUTDOORS   Let shrimp thaw. Reserve six whole shrimp for garnishing. Cut the rest of the shrimp into small pieces. Melt butter, remove from heat, and stir in flour. Return to heat and gradually add milk, stirring constantly over moderate heat until thick. Combine with next seven ingredients. If there is time, chill mixture for easier handling. Shape into patties. Roll shrimpburgers in fine, dry bread crumbs. Fry in about ½ inch of hot fat in a skillet on the grill until browned on one side, about 2 minutes. Turn and brown other side. Serve on toasted hamburger buns with any desired relish or chutney.

INDOORS   Fry shrimpburgers in skillet on the range.
Makes 6 servings.

SOU'WESTER SHRIMP

½ cup oil
½ cup vinegar
⅛ teaspoon paprika
1 envelope spaghetti
  sauce mix

1 pound shrimp, shelled
  and deveined
1 (1-pound) jar stuffed
  green olives
2 large green peppers,
  cubed

OUTDOORS Combine oil, vinegar, paprika, and spaghetti sauce mix. Add shrimp and let stand, covered, in refrigerator for several hours. Before grilling, place shrimp on skewers alternately with olives and green pepper. Grill over charcoal, 8–10 minutes, turning and brushing with remaining marinade.

INDOORS Cook kabobs under broiler 8–10 minutes, brushing as above.
Makes 4 servings.

SHRIMP-MUSHROOM KABOBS

1 pound shrimp, shelled
  and deveined
1 pound medium-sized
  mushrooms
6 tablespoons butter,
  melted

2 tablespoons lemon juice
1 clove garlic, minced
½ teaspoon salt
¼ teaspoon paprika

OUTDOORS Arrange shrimp on skewers alternately with mushroom caps. Combine melted butter, lemon juice, garlic, salt, and paprika. Brush mixture over shrimp. Grill for 10 minutes or until shrimp are pink and tender.

INDOORS Cook kabobs 10 minutes under broiler.
Makes 4–6 servings.

SHRIMP IN FOIL

1 pound shrimp, shelled and deveined
¼ cup canned, sliced mushrooms
⅓ cup butter, melted
2 tablespoons chopped scallions
1 tablespoon chili sauce
⅓ cup chopped parsley
¼ teaspoon salt
¼ teaspoon garlic salt
Few drops Tabasco sauce
Few drops Worcestershire sauce

OUTDOORS   Divide shrimp onto 2 or 3 pieces of aluminum foil (10 x 10 inches); top with mushrooms; turn up edges before adding sauce. To butter, add scallions, chili sauce, parsley, salt, garlic salt, Tabasco sauce, and Worcestershire sauce. Pour over shrimp. Double fold edges to make tightly sealed packets and grill on or close to hot coals 5–10 minutes or until shrimp are done.

INDOORS   Cook packets under the broiler.
Makes 2–3 servings.

BOUILLABAISSE

1 to 2 dozen fresh clams or mussels, in the shell
1 pound shrimp
1½ pounds fish fillets (halibut, cod, sole)
2 tablespoons oil
1 medium onion, chopped
1 clove garlic, crushed
1 (6-ounce) can tomato paste
1 (1-pound) can stewed whole tomatoes
½ teaspoon salt
½ teaspoon sugar
½ teaspoon Tabasco sauce
1 cup water
½ cup white wine (optional)

OUTDOORS   Scrub clam shells well. Shell and devein shrimp. Cut fish into pieces. Heat oil in kettle on grill; add onion and garlic; sauté until tender, about 5 minutes. Add remaining ingredients. If wine is not used, add additional ½ cup water. Bring sauce to a boil; add fish and clams; cover and boil for 2 minutes. Add shrimp and boil 4–6 minutes or until fish flakes easily with a fork.

INDOORS Cook in kettle on the range.
Makes 6 servings.

TROUT BARBECUE

⅓ cup butter
¼ cup water or white wine
1 (8-ounce) can tomato sauce
1 clove garlic, crushed
½ teaspoon dried leaf tarragon

¼ teaspoon sugar
¼ teaspoon Tabasco sauce
¼ teaspoon salt
2 tablespoons lemon juice
4 lake or brook trout (2–4 pounds each), cleaned

OUTDOORS Combine butter, water, tomato sauce, garlic, tarragon, sugar, Tabasco sauce, salt, and lemon juice in a small saucepan. Simmer about 15 minutes. Brush trout generously with sauce. Grill about 10 minutes on each side, brushing frequently with sauce.

INDOORS Cook trout under broiler, brushing as above.
Makes 4–8 servings, depending on size of trout.

GRILLED FILLETS

2 pounds fish fillets (haddock or flounder)
¼ cup lemon juice
2 onions, sliced paper thin
3 tomatoes, sliced

2 tablespoons chopped parsley
1 teaspoon salt
½ teaspoon pepper
½ teaspoon paprika

Trout Barbecue

Whole trout can be cooked right on the grill or under the broiler with taste-tempting results. To add a zesty flavor, brush fish with a homemade sauce before and during cooking. With a clam or oyster stew as a first course, your trout barbecue becomes a banquet from the sea. Courtesy of Tabasco Company

OUTDOORS   Divide fish into 6 portions and arrange in the center of 6 large pieces of aluminum foil. Turn up sides all around. Pour lemon juice over fish in each packet. Place slices of onion and tomato over each portion of fish. Sprinkle with parsley, salt, pepper, and paprika. Fold tops of aluminum foil packets so fish is securely encased in foil. Place on grill for 7–10 minutes, turning packets once during cooking. Test one packet by opening top to see if fish flakes easily with a fork. Roll back tops of foil and serve fish right in the packet.

INDOORS Eliminate foil and place fish in a large baking pan. Season as above and bake in a 350-degree oven for 15 minutes, or until fish flakes easily.
Makes 6 servings.

BARBECUED SNAPPER

2 potatoes, sliced thin
2 onions, sliced thin
2 tomatoes, sliced
4 red snapper fillets, about 2 pounds

½ teaspoon salt
¼ teaspoon pepper
¼ cup lemon juice
4 teaspoons butter

OUTDOORS Using 4 squares of heavy-duty aluminum foil, arrange slices of potatoes, onions, and tomatoes on each square. Top with snapper fillet. Season fillet with salt, pepper, and lemon juice. Dot with butter. Seal tightly and place on grill for 30 minutes, turning packets frequently.

INDOORS Eliminate aluminum foil and place layers of potatoes, onions, tomatoes, and fish in a buttered pan. Season as above. Bake in a 350-degree oven for 20–30 minutes until fish flakes easily with a fork and potatoes are tender.
Makes 4 servings.

GRILLED SALMON STEAKS

4 thick fresh salmon steaks

1 cup French dressing
4 lemon wedges

OUTDOORS Arrange each salmon steak on a double-thick square of aluminum foil, turning up sides all around. Baste fish on all sides with French dressing. Place on hot grill for 20–25 minutes, turning once. Garnish with a wedge of lemon on each steak.

INDOORS Use the broiler.
Makes 4 servings.

TUNA BURGERS

2 (7-ounce) cans tuna in vegetable oil
½ cup chili sauce
¼ cup minced green pepper
2 tablespoons minced onion
½ teaspoon salt
¼ teaspoon Tabasco sauce
6 hamburger buns, sliced
Onion rings (optional)
Pepper rings (optional)

OUTDOORS In medium-size bowl, blend tuna, chili sauce, pepper, onion, salt, and Tabasco sauce. Spoon onto bottom half of hamburger buns; garnish with onion and pepper rings if desired, cover with top of bun. Wrap in aluminum foil; place on grill for about 10 minutes on each side. Serve hot.

INDOORS Use the broiler.
Makes 6 servings.

SCALLOP-BACON KABOBS

1 pound fresh sea scallops
6 strips of bacon
¼ cup soy sauce
2 tablespoons brown sugar

OUTDOORS   Wrap each scallop with ½ slice of bacon. Combine soy sauce and sugar in a shallow bowl. Dip each wrapped scallop in the mixture. Thread on skewers. Place on hot grill for 10 minutes, turning once, until bacon is crisp. Serve hot.

INDOORS   Use the broiler.
Makes 4 servings.

TUNA-SHRIMP STEW

1 (6½-ounce) can tuna, drained	1 (1-pound) can kidney beans and liquid
1 (4½-ounce) can shrimp, drained and cleaned	2 (8-ounce) cans tomato sauce with mushrooms
1 onion, chopped	1 teaspoon chili powder
½ cup sliced celery	¼ teaspoon sugar
	¼ teaspoon salt

OUTDOORS   Combine all ingredients in a large skillet; cover and simmer for 20 minutes over outdoor grill. Serve at once.

INDOORS   Cook in skillet on the range.
Makes 4 servings.

TUNA TOBOGGANS

2 (10½-ounce) cans condensed cheese soup	6 (7-ounce) cans tuna in vegetable oil
2 (10½-ounce) cans condensed cream of mushroom soup	2 (1-pound) cans peas
	1 (4-ounce) can pimiento
	12 hero rolls, split, buttered, and toasted

OUTDOORS Combine soups in large saucepan. Drain peas; reserve ½ cup liquid. Add liquid to soups and stir to blend while heating on the grill. Add tuna, peas, and pimiento. Heat to serving temperature. Spoon over toasted rolls.

INDOORS Cook in saucepan on the range.
   Makes 12 servings.

10/Grate Vegetables

Pick a vegetable. Any vegetable! Wrap it in foil, cleaned, buttered, and seasoned, and pop it on the grill for a nutritious—and delicious—side dish.

When choosing your vegetables, select the colors, tastes, and textures that will best enhance your menu. Insist on good quality fresh vegetables that are firm to the touch and give promise of tenderness.

Treat yourself to the pleasure of ears of fresh corn, soaked in their husks in sugared water and then wrapped in foil and grilled. Later, serve with butter and salt, and you'll have corn-on-the-cob unrivaled by any you have ever eaten. Or try any of the hearty vegetable recipes included here—each designed to be a perfect complement to your next barbecue.

GRILLED BANANAS

6 firm bananas
¼ cup butter, melted

1 tablespoon lemon juice

OUTDOORS   Peel bananas. Brush with melted butter and lemon juice; wrap each banana in a piece of aluminum foil. Grill over hot coals for 10 minutes.

INDOORS   Broil 3–4 inches from heat for 5 minutes on each side or until fork tender.
Makes 6 servings.

CRANBERRY BAKED BEANS

2 cups fresh cranberries
1⅓ cups brown sugar
2 tablespoons lemon juice

1 (1-pound) can baked beans with pork

OUTDOORS   Combine cranberries, 1 cup of the sugar, and the lemon juice in a saucepan; bring to a boil and cook until cranberries begin to pop. Stir occasionally during cooking. Combine beans and remaining ⅓ cup sugar in a 1-quart casserole; top with cranberry mixture. Cover and place on hot grill for about 30 minutes or until mixture is hot and bubbly. Serve with grilled frankfurters or ham.

INDOORS Put casserole in a 375-degree oven for about 30 minutes.
Makes 4 servings.

GREEN BEANS IN FOIL

2 (10-ounce) packages
frozen green beans
¼ cup butter
2 tablespoons minced
onion

1 teaspoon prepared
mustard
½ teaspoon white
horseradish

OUTDOORS Place frozen beans on large, double-thick square of aluminum foil. Mash together butter, onion, mustard, and horseradish; dot beans with this mixture. Wrap foil tightly. Place on a hot grill for about 30 minutes.

INDOORS Bake foil-wrapped beans in a 375-degree oven for about 30 minutes.
Serves 6–8.

ITALIAN GREEN BEANS

2 (10-ounce) packages
frozen green beans
1 medium onion, sliced
thin

½ cup bottled Italian
dressing

OUTDOORS Place frozen beans on a large, double-thick square of aluminum foil. Spread onion rings over beans and turn up sides of foil. Pour Italian dressing over beans. Fold top of foil tightly. Place on a hot grill for 30 minutes. Serve hot.

INDOORS Cook foil-wrapped beans in a 375-degree oven for about 30 minutes.
Makes 6–8 servings.

CHEDDARY CHILI BEANS

1 (15½-ounce) can chili beans
2 cups grated cheddar cheese

¼ cup canned peeled green chili peppers, chopped
½ cup chopped onions

OUTDOORS Mix chili beans, cheddar cheese, peppers, and onions together in a saucepan on the grill. Simmer until thoroughly heated and cheese melts. Serve hot.

INDOORS Cook in saucepan on the range.
Makes 4 servings.

NEW DELHI BEANS

¼ cup butter
2 onions, chopped
1 (1-pound) can whole peeled tomatoes
2 (1-pound) cans garbanzo beans, drained and rinsed

½ (10½-ounce) can beef bouillon
1½ teaspoons turmeric
½ teaspoon ginger
¼ teaspoon dried mint leaves
Dash of cayenne

OUTDOORS Melt butter in large saucepan on the grill. Add onions and cook until transparent. Add tomatoes, garbanzos, bouillon, turmeric, ginger, mint, and cayenne. Cover and simmer until thoroughly heated. Serve piping hot.

INDOORS Cook in saucepan on the range.
Makes 6–8 servings.

LEMON-BUTTERED CABBAGE

¼ cup butter
1 large head cabbage, shredded
½ teaspoon grated lemon rind

2 tablespoons lemon juice
½ teaspoon celery seed
½ teaspoon salt
¼ teaspoon pepper

OUTDOORS   Melt butter in a large skillet over grill. Add shredded cabbage. Cover and cook, stirring occasionally, about 6–8 minutes, or until just tender. Add lemon rind, juice, celery seed, salt, and pepper. Stir. Serve at once.

INDOORS   Cook in skillet on the range.
Makes 6 servings.

CARROT-PINEAPPLE BAKE

2 (1-pound) cans sliced carrots, drained
1 (8-ounce) can crushed pineapple

1 tablespoon brown sugar
2 tablespoons butter

OUTDOORS   Arrange carrot slices on a double-thick, 12-inch square of heavy-duty aluminum foil, turning up edges and making a 6-inch-square packet. Turn up sides and spoon crushed pineapple, sugar, and butter over carrots. Seal foil. Place on a hot grill for 10 minutes, turning packet frequently. Serve hot.

INDOORS   Cook packets in a 350-degree oven for 15 minutes.
Makes 6 servings.

SWEET CORN IN HUSKS

1 quart water
2 tablespoons sugar
8 freshly picked ears of
corn, in husks

3 tablespoons butter
½ teaspoon salt

OUTDOORS   Combine water and sugar. Soak corn in mixture for 15 minutes. Remove and wrap each ear, still in husks, in a square of aluminum foil. Place on the grill and cook for 15 minutes, turning often. Remove foil when ready to serve, strip corn clean of husks, and spread butter and salt over the hot kernels.

INDOORS   Place foil-wrapped corn in a 375-degree oven for 20 minutes.
Makes 8 servings.

HERB-ROASTED CORN

8 ears of corn
¼ pound butter
2 teaspoons monosodium
glutamate

1 teaspoon salt
½ teaspoon pepper
½ teaspoon marjoram

OUTDOORS   Remove husks and silk from ears of corn. Place each ear on double-thick square of aluminum foil. Dot with butter and sprinkle with monosodium glutamate, salt, pepper, and marjoram. Wrap in foil. Roast on hot grill for 20 minutes, turning several times during cooking.

INDOORS   Place foil-wrapped corn in a 375-degree oven for 20 minutes.
Makes 8 servings.

GRILLED EGGPLANT

1 large eggplant
½ cup flour
½ cup butter, melted

½ cup grated Parmesan cheese

OUTDOORS   Peel eggplant and cut lengthwise into ½-inch slices. Dust lightly with flour and brush one side with melted butter. Place buttered side down on a hot grill for 4 minutes, then turn and brush other side with butter before replacing on the grill. Sprinkle each slice with Parmesan cheese just before removing from grill to serve.

INDOORS   Cook eggplant in a large skillet on range.
Makes 6–8 servings.

STUFFED MUSHROOMS

2 tablespoons instant minced onion
1 tablespoon prepared mustard
2 cups prepared mashed potatoes

24 large fresh mushroom caps
¼ cup butter, melted
2 tablespoons parsley flakes

OUTDOORS   Stir onion and mustard into prepared mashed potatoes. Wash mushrooms, removing stems. Brush caps with melted butter and place, stem side down, on foil over hot grill. Grill 2–5 minutes. Turn, brush with butter, and fill with mashed potato mixture. Sprinkle with crushed parsley flakes. Grill 10 minutes or until mushrooms are soft and tender and potatoes are piping hot.

INDOORS   Use the broiler.
Makes 6–8 servings.

KIDNEY KRAUT

2 strips of bacon, diced
¼ cup chopped onion
1 (14-ounce) can
  sauerkraut

2 (15½-ounce) cans dark
  red kidney beans,
  drained and rinsed in
  cold water
1 (12-ounce) can beer
1 teaspoon caraway seeds

OUTDOORS   Sauté bacon in large saucepan on the grill until lightly browned. Add onion and cook until transparent. Add sauerkraut and beans. Pour beer over all and let simmer until heated through and all flavors are well blended. Sprinkle with caraway seeds. Serve piping hot.

INDOORS   Cook in saucepan on the range.
Makes 6 servings.

ONIONS STUFFED WITH PEAS

4 large white onions
2 tablespoons butter
2 tablespoons flour
1 (1-pound) can
  sweet peas
¼ cup heavy cream

1 tablespoon brandy
Dash of cayenne
Dash of nutmeg
¼ teaspoon salt
¼ cup shelled and
  chopped walnuts

OUTDOORS   Peel onions. Cut in half and cut thin slice off ends so they will stand evenly in a flat pan. Boil in salted water 15–25 minutes until just tender but not falling apart. Drain and save ¼ cup liquid. Scoop out centers of onions and discard. Melt butter in 1-quart saucepan; add flour to make paste. Gradually add liquid from can of peas, cream, and brandy. Cook over low heat until thickened. Season with cayenne, nutmeg, and salt. Heat peas in leftover onion liquid until hot. Drain. Mix with walnuts. Stuff onion cavities with

Onions Stuffed with Peas

Create an elegant side dish by boiling onions, scooping out their centers, and filling them with sweet peas and walnuts in a creamy, brandy-flavored sauce. Cook this dish indoors and, if you wish, reheat on the grill alongside your entree. Courtesy of S & W Fine Foods

peas and nut mixture. Pour sauce over all, taking care to let some seep through peas into onion cavities. Arrange in flat pan and reheat on grill before serving.

INDOORS   Serve at once or reheat in a 350-degree oven for 10–15 minutes.
Makes 8 servings.

PEAS AND TOMATOES IN FOIL

2 (10-ounce) packages
  frozen peas
1 onion, sliced thin
2 tomatoes, sliced thin
2 tablespoons butter

1 teaspoon prepared
  mustard
1 teaspoon brown sugar
½ teaspoon salt

OUTDOORS Arrange blocks of frozen peas on a large double-thick square of heavy-duty aluminum foil. Turn up edges of foil. Top peas with thin slices of onion, then with slices of tomato. Combine butter, mustard, sugar, and salt; place dots of this mixture over tomatoes. Seal packet tightly and place on grill for about 30 minutes, turning several times during cooking.

INDOORS Place packet in a 400-degree oven for 30 minutes. *Makes 6 servings.*

SQUASH WITH ORANGE-DILL SAUCE

2 pounds summer crook-
  neck or yellow squash
¼ cup butter, softened
2 tablespoons frozen
  orange juice concentrate,
  thawed, undiluted

1 small onion, sliced
1 teaspoon salt
1 teaspoon dried dillweed

OUTDOORS Scrub squash. Cut slice from stem and blossom ends; do not pare. Cut into ½-inch slices. Arrange in the center of large square of heavy-duty aluminum foil, turning up the sides all around. Mash butter and orange juice concentrate together. Dot over slices of squash. Top with onion slices, salt, and dill. Fold foil into a tightly closed packet and place on the grill for about 20 minutes, turning often.

INDOORS Prepare squash slices as above. Melt butter and orange juice in a skillet, add squash, onions, salt, and dill; cover tightly and cook over moderate heat for 10–15 minutes until squash is tender.
Makes 4–6 servings.

BUFFET POTATOES

1 (1-pound) package frozen French-fried potatoes
3 tablespoons butter
½ cup (2 ounces) shredded sharp processed American cheese

¼ teaspoon salt
⅛ teaspoon pepper
½ cup light cream

OUTDOORS Place potatoes on large double-thick square of heavy-duty aluminum foil and turn up edges. Dot with butter; sprinkle with cheese, salt, and pepper. Pour cream over top. Close package, sealing edges together with a double fold. Heat on grill over medium fire, turning occasionally, for 30 minutes or until potatoes are done.

INDOORS Bake packet in a 375-degree oven for 30 minutes.
Makes 4 servings.

HOT GERMAN POTATO SALAD

½-pound sliced bacon
3 tablespoons sugar
2 tablespoons instant minced onion
1 tablespoon flour
1½ teaspoons salt

½ teaspoon celery seed
¼ teaspoon pepper
½ cup water
⅓ cup vinegar
2 (1-pound) cans sliced potatoes, drained

OUTDOORS   Cut bacon into 1-inch pieces. Cook in skillet on
the grill until crisp; remove and drain, reserving 2 tablespoons drippings. Combine sugar, onion, flour, and seasonings; stir into drippings. Gradually add water and vinegar.
Heat to boiling, stirring constantly. Add potatoes and bacon
pieces. Cook slowly, stirring occasionally, 5 minutes or until
heated through.

INDOORS   Cook in skillet on the range.
Makes 6 servings.

GRILLED POTATOES

2 cups frozen hash brown potatoes	1 tablespoon chopped chives
1/4 cup butter, melted	1 teaspoon dill
1 tablespoon chopped parsley	1/2 teaspoon salt
	1/4 teaspoon monosodium glutamate

OUTDOORS   Simmer and drain potatoes according to package
directions. Combine with remaining ingredients. Wrap tightly in a 15-inch length of aluminum foil. Cook on grill 15–20
minutes, turning occasionally.

INDOORS   Bake packet in a 375-degree oven for 25 minutes.
Makes 4 servings.

ZUCCHINI-TOMATO KABOBS

4 thin zucchini, about 9 inches long	1 teaspoon oregano
32 cherry tomatoes	1/2 teaspoon salt

OUTDOORS Cut each zucchini into 1-inch-thick discs. Thread onto 8 skewers alternately with cherry tomatoes, piercing through the cut sides of the zucchini. Sprinkle with oregano and salt. Place on the grill for 4 or 5 minutes, turning skewers occasionally. Serve hot.

INDOORS Use the broiler.
Makes 8 servings.

BAKED TOMATOES STUFFED WITH SPINACH

6 large tomatoes	½ onion, grated
½ teaspoon salt	2 tablespoons butter
1 (10-ounce) package frozen chopped spinach	¼ teaspoon nutmeg
	¼ cup fine bread crumbs

OUTDOORS Cut a thin slice from the flower end of each tomato; discard. Carefully remove pulp from each tomato; reserve. Sprinkle inside of tomatoes with salt. Cook spinach and grated onion as directed on the package; drain thoroughly. Mix butter and nutmeg through spinach; chop tomato pulp and add. Stuff tomatoes with spinach mixture. Top with bread crumbs. Arrange tomatoes in a small foil-lined pan; place on a hot grill for 15–20 minutes until tomatoes are tender but still hold their shape. Serve hot.

INDOORS Cook stuffed tomatoes in a 350-degree oven.
Makes 6 servings.

11/Cool Salads

Play it cool with salads, but don't ignore the wide range of choices that will enable you to do your own salad thing!

Why settle for the same old lettuce tossed with bottled dressing when you can mix and match a variety of vegetables and fruits with some zesty homemade dressings? Here are potato salads and cole slaws that have extra flavor. You will find aspics and gelatin salads that blend tastefully with hot grilled foods. All will lend color and gusto to your festive board.

To crisp your salad greens to perfection, wash them clean, drain, then roll in paper toweling and refrigerate until ready to use later in the day. They will be chilled and fresh, just waiting for a shower of good dressing!

SPINACH SALAD WITH CHILI-LEMON DRESSING

1 bunch fresh spinach
1 tablespoon lemon juice
2 tablespoons salad oil
¼ teaspoon salt
1 cup mayonnaise
¼ cup chili sauce

1 teaspoon grated lemon rind
Juice of 1 lemon
1 tablespoon finely minced green onion

Wash spinach well; shake gently to dry. Cut off all stems. Tear leaves into bite-size pieces. Sprinkle with lemon juice, oil, and salt; toss to coat spinach. Combine mayonnaise, chili sauce, lemon rind, lemon juice, and onion. Chill until ready to serve and pour over spinach.
Makes 4 servings.

SPINACH-CITRUS SALAD

1 (1-pound) can grapefruit sections, drained
1 teaspoon salt
1 pound fresh spinach, washed and stemmed

1 (4-ounce) can ripe pitted extra large olives
3 tablespoons salad oil
2 tablespoons vinegar

Empty grapefruit sections into a bowl and sprinkle with salt. Let stand for 15 minutes. Tear spinach leaves into a salad

bowl; place salted grapefruit sections and olives on spinach. Pour oil and vinegar over all and toss lightly.
Makes 4–6 servings.

SPINACH-CHIVE SALAD

1 pound fresh spinach leaves
¾ cup dairy sour cream
¼ cup mayonnaise
2 tablespoons chopped chives

2 tablespoons minced parsley
½ clove garlic, minced
4 teaspoons lemon juice
4 teaspoons vinegar
½ teaspoon salt

Wash spinach leaves in cold water. Drain on absorbent paper and blot dry. Combine remaining ingredients for dressing; add to spinach leaves and toss lightly.
Makes 4 servings.

CARROT-SESAME SLAW

1 (1-pound) can julienne carrots, drained
2 cups shredded crisp raw cabbage
1 tablespoon chopped onion
1 tablespoon chopped green pepper

¼ cup dairy sour cream
¼ cup mayonnaise
1 teaspoon prepared mustard
1 tablespoon toasted sesame seeds

Place carrots, cabbage, onion, and green pepper in salad bowl. Combine sour cream, mayonnaise, and mustard. Pour over carrot-cabbage mixture. Sprinkle with sesame seeds.
Makes 4 servings.

GARDEN COLE SLAW

1½ cups shredded cabbage
1 (8½-ounce) can sweet
  peas, drained
½ cup diced cucumber
½ cup diced celery
¼ cup chopped green
  pepper
1 teaspoon salt

½ cup dairy sour cream
1 tablespoon white
  wine vinegar
4 teaspoons sugar
¼ teaspoon prepared
  mustard
Paprika

Combine vegetables in medium-size bowl; sprinkle with salt.
Mix sour cream, vinegar, sugar, and mustard; spoon over
salad, tossing lightly. Chill; sprinkle with paprika.
Makes 6 servings.

ZIPPY POTATO SALAD

4 cups diced cooked
  potatoes
¼ cup chopped celery
¼ cup sliced olives
2 hard-cooked eggs,
  chopped
2 tablespoons chopped
  onion
¾ cup mayonnaise

¼ cup Italian-style dressing
2 tablespoons prepared
  mustard
1 teaspoon prepared
  horseradish
½ teaspoon salt
1 (17-ounce) can small
  early peas, drained

Combine potatoes with celery, olives, eggs, and onion; toss
lightly. Blend mayonnaise with Italian-style dressing, mustard,
horseradish, and salt. Pour over potato mixture along with
drained canned peas. Toss lightly. Chill thoroughly.
Makes 6 servings.

SUNNY POTATO SALAD

6 medium-size potatoes,
cooked and diced
½ cup chopped celery
¼ cup chopped onion
3 hard-cooked eggs,
chopped
1 cup dairy sour cream

½ cup mayonnaise
2 tablespoons vinegar
1 tablespoon prepared
yellow mustard
¾ teaspoon salt
½ teaspoon black pepper

Combine potatoes, celery, onion, and eggs. Separately, combine sour cream, mayonnaise, vinegar, mustard, salt, and pepper. Toss vegetables with dressing until well blended. Refrigerate several hours before serving.
Makes 8 servings.

FIRECRACKER POTATO SALAD

1 envelope seasoning
mix for Sloppy Joes
¼ cup water
3 tablespoons prepared
yellow mustard
1¼ cups mayonnaise

½ cup sweet pickle relish
6 cups cubed cooked
potatoes
1 cup diced celery
6 hard-cooked eggs
Lettuce leaves (optional)

Combine seasoning mix and water in large bowl; let stand a few minutes for water to be absorbed. Add mustard, mayonnaise, pickle relish, potatoes, celery, and 4 of the eggs, diced. Toss gently; cover and chill for several hours. Line a bowl with crisp lettuce leaves, if desired. Fill bowl with potato salad; garnish with remaining 2 eggs, sliced.
Makes 8 servings.

CHINESE VEGETABLE SALAD

1 (1-pound) can fancy mixed Chinese vegetables
¾ cup chopped green onion
1 small head of lettuce, torn in bite-size pieces
1 cup shredded cabbage
¾ cup bottled creamy garlic dressing

Drain mixed vegetables and rinse with cold water; drain thoroughly and chill. Add onion, lettuce, and cabbage. Toss with creamy garlic dressing.
Makes 6–8 servings.

SEAFOOD CAESAR

6 cups salad greens, torn in bite-size pieces
¾ cup croutons
1 avocado, peeled and diced
1 tomato, peeled and cut in wedges
2 cups cooked seafood (shrimp, lobster, or crab meat)
¾ cup prepared Caesar dressing

Place salad greens, croutons, avocado, tomato, and seafood in a salad bowl. Add Caesar dressing and toss lightly.
Makes 4–6 servings.

CHEF SALAD

1 head lettuce, torn in bite-size pieces
2 tomatoes, cut in wedges
1 jar pickled artichoke hearts, including oil
¼ pound boiled ham, cut in long strips
¼ pound Swiss cheese, cut in long strips
¼ cup chopped chives
Oil and vinegar dressing

Combine torn lettuce with tomato wedges and artichoke hearts. Top with strips of ham and Swiss cheese. Sprinkle with chopped chives. Serve with oil and vinegar dressing.
Makes 4–6 servings.

BARBECUE BEAN SALAD

1 (1-pound) can French-cut green beans
1 (1-pound) can yellow wax beans
1 (1-pound) can red kidney beans
½ cup thinly sliced red onion
1 green pepper, slivered

½ cup salad oil
⅔ cup wine vinegar or cider vinegar
1 tablespoon Worcestershire sauce
½ cup sugar
½ teaspoon salt
Lettuce leaves

Drain canned beans well. Combine beans, onion, and green pepper. Mix salad oil, vinegar, Worcestershire sauce, sugar, and salt. Pour over vegetables and chill several hours or overnight, stirring occasionally. Drain and serve on lettuce.
Makes 6–8 servings.

ORANGE-HAM RING SALAD

2 eggs
¼ teaspoon Tabasco sauce
1 teaspoon dry mustard
2 cups dry bread crumbs
2½ cups ground cooked ham
2½ cups ground cooked veal

1 (6-ounce) can frozen orange juice concentrate, thawed, undiluted
½ cup water
Lettuce leaves

Beat eggs in large bowl. Stir in Tabasco sauce and mustard. Add bread crumbs, ground ham, veal, orange juice concentrate, and water; mix well. Press meat mixture into a 6-cup ring mold. Bake in a 350-degree oven for 1 hour. Turn out onto serving platter. Cool. Garnish with lettuce leaves. *Makes 8 servings.*

BEET-ORANGE SALAD

1 (11-ounce) can Mandarin oranges, chilled
½ cup olive oil
1 tablespoon wine vinegar
½ teaspoon salt

⅛ teaspoon pepper
1 bunch curly endive lettuce
1 (1-pound) can julienne beets, chilled and drained

Drain Mandarin oranges, reserving 1 tablespoon syrup. Put oil, vinegar, syrup from oranges, salt, pepper, and 6 orange segments in blender; blend well. Arrange lettuce, beets, and remaining oranges in a salad bowl. Pour dressing over salad mixture. *Makes 6 servings.*

MACARONI PETAL SALAD

1 (7-ounce) package macaroni
¾ cup mayonnaise
2 tablespoons onion soup mix
¼ teaspoon salt
1 (17-ounce) can sweet peas, drained

1 cup cubed cheddar cheese
½ cup chopped celery
2 tablespoons chopped pimiento
6 bologna slices, halved

Macaroni Petal Salad

For the perfect complement to your next barbecue try this delicious and decorative salad, which combines seasoned macaroni, cheese, peas, celery, and pimiento. Top with bologna slices, as shown. Courtesy of Green Giant Company

Cook macaroni according to package directions. Combine with mayonnaise blended with onion soup mix and salt. Lightly mix in drained peas, cheese, celery, and pimiento. Spoon into serving dish. Arrange bologna in an upright position in concentric circles on top of salad. Chill thoroughly. *Makes 6 servings.*

AVOCADO-CITRUS SALAD

1 (1-pound) can grapefruit
sections
1 (11-ounce) can
Mandarin orange
sections
1 head lettuce, torn
into bite-size pieces
1 avocado, peeled
and sliced

1 cucumber, sliced paper
thin
½ cup salad oil
2 tablespoons sugar
2 tablespoons cider
vinegar
¼ teaspoon salt

Drain grapefruit and orange sections, reserving juice. Combine grapefruit and orange sections with lettuce, avocado, and cucumber in a large salad bowl. Add salad oil to ½ cup combined reserved fruit juices; add sugar, vinegar, and salt. Pour fruit dressing over salad just before serving.
Makes 6–8 servings.

PINEAPPLE-CUCUMBER MOLDED SALAD

1 cup crushed pineapple,
with syrup
1 (3-ounce) package
lemon-flavored gelatin
½ teaspoon salt
½ cup finely grated carrots
1 (3-ounce) package lime-
flavored gelatin
½ cup hot water

1 cup mayonnaise
½ cup dairy sour cream
½ teaspoon salt
1 tablespoon grated onion
½ cup finely chopped
celery
½ cup grated cucumber,
drained
Salad greens

Drain pineapple; add enough water to syrup to make 1¾ cups liquid. Heat to boiling; add lemon gelatin and stir to dissolve. Add salt, carrots, and crushed pineapple; turn into a 1½-quart ring mold and chill until firm. Then dissolve lime gelatin in hot water; add mayonnaise, sour cream, salt, onion, celery, and cucumber. Pour over firm pineapple layer and chill until firm. Unmold and garnish with salad greens. *Makes 8–10 servings.*

SHRIMP AND ASPIC SALAD

1 (3-ounce) package lemon-flavored gelatin
¾ cup hot water
1 can tomato sauce
2 tablespoons vinegar
¾ teaspoon salt
Dash of pepper
1 head iceberg lettuce
1½ cups cooked shrimp, chilled
1 cup shredded Mozzarella or Swiss cheese
½ cup sliced ripe olives
1 cup dairy sour cream
¼ cup finely chopped celery
¼ cup catsup
2 tablespoons sweet pickle relish
1 tablespoon lemon juice

Dissolve gelatin in hot water. Add tomato sauce, vinegar, ½ teaspoon salt, and pepper. Pour into 8-inch-square shallow pan and chill until firm. Break up lettuce and toss with shrimp, shredded cheese, and olives. Cut tomato aspic into 1-inch squares and add to salad; toss very gently. Serve salad with dressing made by blending together the sour cream, celery, catsup, pickle relish, lemon juice, and remaining ¼ teaspoon salt.
Makes 4–6 servings.

SEASIDE ASPIC MOLD

1 (16-ounce) can Clamato juice
1 package unflavored gelatin
1 tablespoon lemon juice
1 cup cooked shrimp
2 tablespoons chopped onion
2 tablespoons chopped green pepper
Unpeeled cucumber slices, scored

Pour Clamato juice in saucepan; stir gelatin into cold Clamato juice to soften, then heat, stirring, to dissolve completely. Chill until slightly thickened. Add lemon juice, shrimp, onion, and green pepper. Rinse a 3-cup mold with cold water. Spoon in gelatin mixture. Slip in a row of cucumber slices around outer edge of mold. Return to refrigerator and chill until firm. At serving time, unmold and garnish with cucumber slices.
Makes 6 servings.

TOMATO-DILL ASPIC

2 (3-ounce) packages seasoned tomato-flavored gelatin
1 cup boiling water
3 cups tomato juice
2 teaspoons vinegar
1 tablespoon grated onion
¼ teaspoon salt

⅓ cup chopped green pepper
½ cup chopped stuffed olives
¾ cup chopped celery
1 teaspoon dried dillweed
1 (17-ounce) can sweet peas, drained

Dissolve gelatin in boiling water. Add tomato juice and chill until partially thickened. Add remaining ingredients. Place in well-oiled 2-quart mold; chill until firm.
Makes 8–10 servings.

MAURICE SALAD DRESSING

¼ cup mayonnaise
⅓ cup lemon juice
2 cups salad oil
1 teaspoon salt
1 teaspoon instant meat tenderizer

½ teaspoon dry mustard
½ teaspoon paprika
4 scallions (including tops), sliced thinly

Combine mayonnaise, lemon juice, and salad oil. Add salt, tenderizer, mustard, paprika, and scallions. Beat thoroughly. *Makes about 2½ cups.*

CREAM CHEESE-CITRUS DRESSING

1 (3-ounce) package
cream cheese, softened
2 tablespoons firmly
packed brown sugar
1 tablespoon grated
orange rind

¼ cup fresh orange juice
1½ tablespoons fresh
lemon juice
½ cup salad oil
½ teaspoon salt
¼ teaspoon paprika

Cream together softened cheese and sugar. Add remaining ingredients, mixing well.
Makes about 1¼ cups.

CALIFORNIA DRESSING

1 orange, peeled, cut in
small pieces
1 (15-ounce) can sweetened
condensed milk
1 tablespoon grated
lemon rind

½ cup lemon juice
¼ teaspoon salt
½ teaspoon prepared
mustard
½ teaspoon curry powder

Place orange pieces in electric blender; add half the sweetened condensed milk. Mix on low speed until mixture is smooth and well blended. Add remaining ingredients; blend on low speed until well mixed. Chill.
Makes 2 cups.

12/Warm Bread

A loaf of bread, herbed and buttered, wrapped in foil, and heated through is a simple way to stimulate appetites. Keep in mind these easy tricks and the staff of life could well become the life of your party!

Always cut a whole bread to within an inch of the bottom crust so pieces can be broken off with ease at serving time.

Spread with seasonings and foil wrap to hold the bread together and prevent it from charring. Heat just long enough to warm through, as too much heat will dry the loaf and make it hard. Peel back the foil at serving time, leaving enough around the bread to retain the heat for second servings.

Try the flavorful ideas in this chapter, and there'll be nothing left of your hot bread but the crumbs!

HOT BUTTERED CHEESE BREAD

1 long loaf Italian bread	2 tablespoons grated
¼ pound butter	Parmesan cheese
	1 teaspoon oregano

OUTDOORS   Cut diagonal slices across the bread, being careful to stop before cutting completely through the bottom of the bread. Soften butter and blend with grated cheese and oregano. Spread between slices. Wrap bread in aluminum foil. Place on the grill for 5–10 minutes. Peel back aluminum foil and serve hot.

INDOORS   Place foil-wrapped bread in a 350-degree oven for 5–10 minutes.
Makes about 12 servings.

HOT BUTTERED GARLIC BREAD

1 long loaf French bread	2 cloves garlic, crushed
¼ pound butter	

OUTDOORS   Cut diagonal slices across the bread, being careful to stop before cutting completely through the bottom of the bread. Soften butter and blend with garlic. Spread mixture between slices. Wrap bread in aluminum foil. Place on the grill for about 5 minutes, or until heated through. Peel back aluminum foil and serve hot.

INDOORS   Place foil-wrapped bread in a 350-degree oven for 5–10 minutes.
Makes about 12 servings.

HOT BUTTERED ONION BREAD

1 long loaf French bread   2 tablespoons dried onion
¼ pound butter   soup mix

OUTDOORS   Cut diagonal slices across the bread, being careful to stop before cutting completely through the bottom of the bread. Soften butter and blend with dried onion soup mix. Spread mixture between slices. Wrap bread in aluminum foil. Place on the grill for 5–10 minutes. Peel back aluminum foil and serve hot.

INDOORS   Place foil-wrapped bread in a 350-degree oven for 5–10 minutes.
Makes about 12 servings.

HOT CHEDDAR CHEESE BREAD

1 long loaf French bread   ¾ cup grated cheddar
¼ cup butter   cheese

OUTDOORS   Cut diagonal slices across the bread, being careful to stop before cutting completely through the bottom of the bread. Soften butter and blend with grated cheese. Spread mixture between slices. Wrap bread in aluminum foil. Place on the grill for 10 minutes, or until heated through enough to melt cheese. Peel back aluminum foil and serve hot.

INDOORS Place foil-wrapped bread in a 350-degree oven for 10 minutes.
Makes about 12 servings.

SESAME-CHEESE LOAF

1/4 pound softened butter	1 long loaf French bread
1 envelope cheese sauce mix	2 tablespoons sesame seed

OUTDOORS Blend together butter and sauce mix. Cut bread in half, lengthwise. Spread cheese mixture on cut surface; sprinkle with sesame seed. Cut bread diagonally in 1½-inch slices, not quite through the bottom crust. Wrap in foil; heat on grill for 10 minutes or until piping hot.

INDOORS Place foil-wrapped bread in a 350-degree oven for 10 minutes.
Makes about 12 servings.

CORNY CORN BREAD

1 package corn bread mix	2 tablespoons dried parsley flakes
1 (8-ounce) can kernel corn, drained	

Prepare corn bread mix according to directions on the package, using the prescribed added ingredients. Add the drained corn and parsley flakes, mixing well. Pour into a 9-inch-square greased pan and bake according to directions on the package. Serve hot.
Makes 12 servings.

CARAWAY CRESCENTS

1 package refrigerator
  crescent rolls
2 tablespoons caraway
  seeds

1 egg yolk
1 tablespoon water

Unroll dough and separate into 8 triangles. Sprinkle with caraway seeds, reserving about 2 teaspoons of seeds for topping. Reroll each triangle into a crescent shape, starting with the wide side of triangle and rolling to the point. Mix egg yolk and water; brush on tops of rolls and sprinkle with remaining caraway seeds. Bake according to directions on the package, or in a 375-degree oven until browned. Reheat on the grill by wrapping in aluminum foil and placing on the rim of the grill about five minutes before serving. *Makes 8 servings.*

ONION CRESCENT ROLLS

1 package refrigerator
  crescent rolls
2 tablespoons dried
  onion soup mix

1 egg yolk
1 tablespoon water
2 teaspoons coarse salt

Unroll dough and separate into 8 triangles. Sprinkle with dried onion soup mix. Reroll each triangle into a crescent shape, starting with the wide side of triangle and rolling to the point. Mix egg yolk and water; brush on tops of rolls and sprinkle each with about 1/4 teaspoon coarse salt. Bake according to package directions, or in a 375-degree oven until browned. Reheat on the grill by wrapping in aluminum foil and placing on the rim of grill about five minutes before serving. *Makes 8 servings.*

13 / Delicious Desserts

Whether your dessert is impromptu or makes a long planned entrance doesn't matter at all. It's the taste that counts.

Here are some quick tricks that will win you applause. You can take ordinary ice cream from the freezer and add hot sauce right off the grill to create some unique sundaes. Or serve a chocolate barbecue boat that heats chocolate bits and marshmallows between layers of cookies that will make your sweet tooth grin for hours!

Baked apples and other fruit take kindly to a grilling, if protected by foil and seasoned with sugar and spices and everything nicest! Your biggest problem will be to save these goodies for dessert as greedy hands stretch forth before the meal's end. Fill them with other things and all will have a happy ending!

BAKED APPLES ON THE GRILL

6 large baking apples	¼ teaspoon cinnamon
2 tablespoons butter	⅛ teaspoon nutmeg
1 tablespoon brown sugar	

OUTDOORS　Wash and core apples. Place a teaspoon of butter in each cored cavity. Combine sugar, cinnamon, and nutmeg and place about ½ teaspoon of the mixture into each cavity. Wrap baking apples in foil and place on the hot grill for about 30 minutes, or until they are fork tender. Pour cream into the cavities when you serve, if desired.

INDOORS　Bake foil-wrapped apples in a 350-degree oven for about 25 minutes and test for doneness.
Makes 6 servings.

PICNIC POUND CAKE

1 (1-pound, 1-ounce) package pound cake mix	1 tablespoon grated orange rind
½ cup seedless raisins	2 teaspoons nutmeg
½ cup chopped walnuts	3 tablespoons confectioners sugar

Prepare cake mix according to package directions. Mix in raisins, walnuts, orange rind, and nutmeg. Bake as directed. Let cake cool, then sprinkle sugar over top.
Makes 1 loaf, 10–12 servings.

CHOCOLATE BANANA FREEZI-POPS

6 fully ripe bananas

1 (6-ounce) package semi-sweet chocolate morsels

Peel bananas; cut in half crosswise. Insert a wooden stick into the end of each. Place in a shallow pan; freeze 2–3 hours. Melt semisweet chocolate morsels over hot (not boiling) water. Spread melted chocolate with spatula or knife over each banana. Chocolate will harden immediately. Wrap each banana in aluminum foil; store in freezer.
Makes 12 pops.

MARSHMALLOW KABOBS

24 marshmallows
1 (1-pound) can pineapple chunks, drained

¼ cup coconut flakes

OUTDOORS   Dip marshmallows in reserved pineapple juice. Alternate marshmallows and pineapple chunks rolled in coconut on 8 skewers. Arrange high over a hot grill and cook until marshmallows are lightly browned. Serve at once.

INDOORS   Use broiler.
Makes 8 servings.

CHOCOLATE BARBECUE BOATS

30 vanilla wafer cookies
½ cup raspberry jam

24 miniature marshmallows
1 (7-ounce) package semi-sweet chocolate morsels

OUTDOORS For each "boat" prepare an aluminum foil container 5–6 inches long with 1-inch sides. Pinch ends together. Stack 5 vanilla wafers, spreading jam between them. Place stack on side in foil container. Separate wafers and insert 1 miniature marshmallow and several semisweet chocolate morsels in the jam between the wafers. Place foil "boats" over low heat until marshmallows and chocolate are softened, approximately 10 minutes.

INDOORS Place "boats" on a cookie sheet in a 300-degree oven for 10 minutes.
Makes 6 servings.

BUTTERSCOTCH DAINTIES

2 (6-ounce) packages butterscotch morsels
¾ cup sifted confectioners sugar
½ cup dairy sour cream

1 teaspoon grated orange rind
¼ teaspoon salt
2¼ cups vanilla wafer crumbs
½ cup chopped nuts

Melt butterscotch morsels in top of double boiler over hot (not boiling) water. Remove from water. Add sugar, sour cream, orange rind, and salt; mix well. Blend in vanilla wafer crumbs. Press into waxed-paper-lined 8-inch-square pan. Sprinkle nuts over candy and press gently into surface. Chill until firm. Cut into 1½-inch-by-1-inch pieces.
Makes 40 pieces.

Chocolate Barbecue Boats

These aluminum-foil boats are packed with treats to please every dessert-lover: vanilla wafers, raspberry jam, chocolate morsels, and miniature marshmallows. Heat through until chocolate and marshmallows are soft, and serve right in the foil containers.
Courtesy of Nestle Company

FUDGE-NUT SAUCE

½ cup chopped nuts
2 tablespoons butter,
   melted

1 (6-ounce) package semi-
   sweet chocolate morsels
¾ cup evaporated milk

OUTDOORS   Add nuts to melted butter and cook over medium heat, stirring constantly, until lightly browned. Remove from heat. Stir in semisweet chocolate morsels until melted. Gradually add evaporated milk, stirring until blended. Serve warm or cool over ice cream.

INDOORS Heat on range, stirring constantly.
Makes 1⅔ cups.

BUTTERSCOTCH-RAISIN SAUCE

1 (6-ounce) package
    butterscotch morsels

½ cup evaporated milk
½ cup seedless raisins

OUTDOORS Combine butterscotch morsels and evaporated milk in saucepan and place on medium heat, stirring constantly, until smooth. Remove from heat. Stir in raisins. Serve warm or cool over ice cream.

INDOORS Heat on range, stirring constantly.
Makes 1¼ cups.

SNOWBALLS WITH CARIBBEAN SAUCE

1 (3½-ounce) can flaked
    coconut
1 quart vanilla ice cream
½ cup butter
½ cup sugar

½ cup unsulphured
    molasses
½ cup evaporated milk
2 tablespoons rum
    flavoring (optional)

OUTDOORS Spread coconut in small, shallow pan. Scoop ice cream into 8 balls and roll in coconut. Transfer to foil-lined shallow pan; freeze. Meanwhile, melt butter in saucepan; add sugar and unsulphured molasses. Bring to a full rolling boil, stirring occasionally. Reduce heat and boil 2 minutes, stirring constantly. Remove from heat; stir in evaporated milk and rum flavoring. Reheat on grill and spoon over ice cream balls.

INDOORS   Heat on range, stirring constantly.
Makes 8 servings with 1⅔ cups sauce.

WALNUT-ORANGE SUNDAE

4 egg yolks
½ cup sugar
¾ cup orange juice

1 (11-ounce) can
   Mandarin oranges,
   drained
½ cup chopped walnuts

In top of double boiler, beat egg yolks until light. Beat in sugar and orange juice. Cook over simmering water for 10 minutes, beating constantly with wire whisk or rotary beater, until sauce is thick and custardy. Set the pan in a bowl of ice water and continue beating until sauce is cold. Chill until serving time. At serving time, fold in oranges and walnuts. To serve, spoon over ice cream.
Makes 2½ cups.

GRAPEFRUIT SHERBET

1 (10-ounce) can
   grapefruit juice
½ teaspoon ginger
32 large marshmallows
¼ cup lemon juice

4 egg whites
6 tablespoons sugar
1 (1-pound) can
   grapefruit sections

Combine grapefruit juice, ginger, and marshmallows in a saucepan and heat over low heat, folding in marshmallows until they are half melted. Add lemon juice and continue folding until smooth. Beat egg whites until they are stiff. Gradually beat in sugar; fold egg whites into marshmallow mixture. Pour into refrigerator tray or mold; freeze until firm. Stir occasionally. Decorate with grapefruit sections. *Makes about 12 servings.*

PINEAPPLE BOMBE

1 (1-pound, 4-ounce) can crushed pineapple
3 cups miniature marshmallows
1 teaspoon vanilla extract
⅛ teaspoon almond extract
⅛ teaspoon salt
½ cup chopped toasted pecans
2 quarts vanilla ice cream

Combine undrained pineapple with marshmallows, vanilla and almond extracts, and salt. Cook, stirring occasionally, over low heat until marshmallows are melted. Remove from heat. Cool. Add nuts and chill. Line bottom and sides of chilled 7-cup mixing bowl with two thirds of ice cream. Spoon pineapple mixture into center; cover with remaining ice cream. Cover bowl with foil. Freeze overnight. When ready to serve, unmold on chilled plate. Decorate as desired with rosettes of tinted whipped cream, stemmed maraschino cherries, and canned pineapple chunks.
Makes 8–10 servings.

ICE CREAM BASKET PIE

1 (6-ounce) package semi-sweet chocolate morsels
2 tablespoons shortening
2 cups ready-to-eat crisp rice cereal
½ cup chopped walnuts
1 quart ice cream

Fit a piece of aluminum foil inside and over rim of a 9-inch pie plate, smoothing with fingers to make a liner; trim off excess corners with scissors. Turn semisweet chocolate morsels into plate; add shortening. Heat in a 350-degree oven for 3 minutes. Remove from oven; blend morsels and shortening with back of teaspoon. Stir in crisp rice cereal and walnuts. Spread mixture over bottom, up sides, and over the rim of pie plate to form a shell. Chill until set. Invert pie plate and carefully peel foil from shell; slip into pie plate. Fill with ice cream and chill until ready to serve. Cut into wedges and serve immediately.
Makes 6–8 servings.

NO-BAKE CHEESE PIE

Filling:

1 envelope unflavored gelatin	1 pound cream cheese
½ cup sugar	1 teaspoon lemon rind
⅛ teaspoon salt	1 tablespoon lemon juice
1 cup milk	1 cup heavy cream, whipped

Mix together gelatin, sugar, and salt in a saucepan. Stir in milk. Place over low heat, stirring constantly, until gelatin is dissolved, about 3 minutes. Remove from heat. Cool. (While mixture is cooling, prepare crumb shell below.) Beat cream cheese, lemon rind, and lemon juice together on high speed of electric mixer. Gradually beat in gelatin mixture. Chill until mixture mounds, about 15 minutes. Then fold in whipped cream. Fill crumb shell. Chill until firm.
Makes 8 servings.

Crumb Shell:

1¼ cups graham cracker crumbs	½ teaspoon cinnamon
¼ cup sugar	½ teaspoon nutmeg
	¼ cup butter, softened

Thoroughly blend all ingredients. Press mixture firmly into an even layer against bottom and sides of a 9-inch pie plate.

FLAMING BANANAS MELBA

1 package frozen
raspberries
½ cup currant jelly
1½ teaspoons cornstarch
1 tablespoon cold water
4 firm bananas

¼ cup sweet butter
2 tablespoons Cointreau
½ cup light brown sugar
⅓ cup brandy
2 tablespoons slivered
almonds

Prepare melba sauce in advance by mashing raspberries in a saucepan; add jelly and bring to a boil. Mix cornstarch with water and add to berries. Stir and cook until clear. Chill. Peel bananas and cut in half crosswise. Melt butter in a hot chafing dish, arrange bananas in it, and sprinkle with Cointreau and sugar. Turn the bananas and baste occasionally until lightly browned. Add warmed brandy and set ablaze. Serve with a sprinkling of slivered almonds and melba sauce. *Makes 4 servings.*

BUTTERSCOTCH-ORANGE CHIFFON PIE

1 envelope unflavored
gelatin
1¼ cups orange juice
1 (6-ounce) package
butterscotch morsels
¼ teaspoon salt
4 eggs, separated

1 tablespoon grated
orange rind
½ cup sugar
1 9-inch baked pastry
shell or crumb crust
(see page 143)

Sprinkle gelatin over orange juice in saucepan to soften. Add butterscotch morsels and salt. Place over low heat; stir constantly until gelatin dissolves and morsels melt, about 10 minutes. Gradually stir in slightly beaten egg yolks. Cook over low heat until mixture becomes slightly thickened. Remove from heat; stir in orange rind. Chill, stirring occasionally, until mixture mounds slightly when dropped from a spoon. Beat egg whites until stiff, but not dry. Gradually add sugar and beat until very stiff. Fold in butterscotch mixture. Turn into pastry shell or crumb crust. Chill until firm. If desired, garnish with whipped cream.

Makes 8 servings.

14 / Refreshing Drinks

Liquid refreshment, especially punch, is scheduled for a command performance on any barbecue occasion! Whether served from a pitcher into paper cups or dipped from a bowl into crystal cups, an icy fruit-flavored drink is a treat for any audience. It cools off the spicy aftertaste of hot foods and sets the stage for second helpings.

Use your imagination to present your drink in a more refreshing way! Earlier in the day, mold some clean, fresh flowers in a ring of ice, or tuck a cherry into each ice cube before freezing, and you will have a pretty way of chilling your mixture. Rub the rim of your cups with fresh lemon peel and dip them gently in powdered sugar before pouring in the punch. Add a sprig of fresh mint to some brews and a cinnamon stick to stir others.

Here are a variety of flavorful concoctions: one uses apple, pineapple, and grapefruit juice to make an Apple Polisher's Punch and another mixes citrus juices into a refreshing Citrus Fizz. Just two of many ways of being beaten to the punch!

SEAGOING BLOODY MARY

1 (1½-ounce) jigger clam juice
1 jigger tomato juice
1 jigger vodka (or extra tomato juice)
2 dashes of Worcestershire sauce

Cracked ice
Salt
Pepper
Cayenne
Lemon wedge

Pour clam juice, tomato juice, and vodka over cracked ice in an old-fashioned glass; add seasonings to taste; garnish with lemon.
Makes 1 serving.

PINEAPPLE-GRAPEFRUIT PUNCH

1 (46-ounce) can pineapple-grapefruit juice
1 (1-quart) grape juice

1 large bottle ginger ale
Ice cubes
1 lemon, sliced thin

Combine fruit juices in punch bowl. Pour in chilled ginger ale just before serving time. Add ice cubes and float thin slices of lemon on top.
Makes about 3½ quarts.

CITRUS FIZZ

1 (6-ounce) can frozen orange juice concentrate, thawed, undiluted

¼ cup frozen grapefruit juice concentrate, thawed, undiluted

¼ cup frozen limeade concentrate, thawed, undiluted

1 quart ginger ale
Ice cubes

Blend undiluted concentrates in a large pitcher. Just before serving, add chilled ginger ale and ice. Pour into 6 tall glasses. If desired, decorate with orange wedges and other fruit on food picks.
Makes 6 servings.

STRAWBERRY PINK LEMONADE

2 (12-ounce) cans frozen pink lemonade concentrate

2 quarts water

1 quart ginger ale

1 (12-ounce) package frozen sliced strawberries

1 lemon, sliced paper thin
Ice cubes

Empty lemonade into punch bowl. Add water. Just before serving, add chilled ginger ale and partially thawed sliced strawberries. Add lemon slices and ice cubes.
Makes about 1 gallon.

APPLE POLISHER'S PUNCH

1 quart apple juice
1 quart pineapple-
   grapefruit juice
1 quart grape juice

1 quart ginger ale
Ice cubes
Cinnamon sticks

Combine chilled apple juice, pineapple-grapefruit juice, and grape juice. Just before serving, add chilled ginger ale and ice cubes. Serve with a cinnamon stick stirrer.
Makes 1 gallon.

CITRUS PUNCH

1 quart orange juice
1 quart pineapple juice
1 quart lemon-lime
   carbonated beverage

1 pint lemon sherbet
Ice cubes
Mint leaves

Combine chilled orange juice and pineapple juice in punch bowl. Just before serving add chilled lemon-lime carbonated beverage. Float a mound of lemon sherbet in the punch, add ice cubes, and garnish with fresh mint leaves.
Makes over 3 quarts.

CRANAPPLE PUNCH

Juice of 3 lemons
3 cups sugar
Fresh mint leaves
2 cups water

1 quart cranberry-apple
   juice
1 quart club soda, chilled
Ice cubes
Lemon slices

Combine lemon juice, sugar, 20 small mint leaves, and water. Bring to a boil and simmer 5 minutes. Cool; then strain. Chill. Combine this mint syrup with cranberry-apple juice and club soda in punch bowl. Add ice cubes. Garnish with lemon slices and more mint leaves. Serve in chilled punch cups.
Makes 12–14 punch-cup servings.

CRANBERRY CAPUCINE

¼ cup instant coffee
3 cups cranberry juice, chilled

½ cup heavy cream, whipped
Grated orange rind

Beat coffee into cranberry juice. Chill. Sweeten mixture to taste, if desired. When ready to serve, pour into 6 cups or glasses, top with whipped cream and grated orange rind. Serve at once.
Serves 6.

HOT CHOCOLATE PUNCH

1½ cups quick chocolate-flavored mix

8 cups hot milk
½ cup whipped cream

Put chocolate-flavored mix into a 3-quart punch bowl. Gradually add 1 cup hot milk, stirring until blended. Stir in the rest of the hot milk. Top with spoonfuls of whipped cream.
Makes 8 servings.

Hot Chocolate Punch

For a wintertime barbecue, fill your punch bowl with easy-to-prepare hot chocolate and top with spoonfuls of whipped cream. It's an especially attractive drink to serve along with desserts.
Courtesy of Nestle Company

15 / Guide to Outdoor Equipment

TYPES OF GRILLS

BUILT-INS

These can be set permanently into brick, stone, or cinder block construction. Units are available that use charcoal briquets or permanently fired ceramic rocks that are heated by gas or electric connections. These ceramic rock units are gaining in popularity since they are easy to use and do not detract from the "outdoor" taste of the food. Look for features such as adjustable grids and fire pans, rotisserie spits, and heat controls.

PORTABLES

A variety of models are available, from the simple round brazier to the more elaborate wagon. Extra features on the more expensive models include hoods to protect from wind and to preserve heat, rotisserie spits, adjustable grids and fire pans, and extensive work and storage space. Better models feature chrome-plated grids and ventilated fire pans. Some have completely closed hoods for smoking foods.

HIBACHIS

These range in size from a tiny portable for individual use to double-grill models for more extensive cooking. They are usually constructed of black cast iron. Preferable features are adjustable drafts, greaseless grids, and adjustable controls. Hibachis are interesting to use for individual hors d'oeuvres and kabob cookery.

MAKESHIFT GRILLS

You can place an oven grate between two cinder blocks or across two piles of bricks, and place a bed of sand underneath. This method is expedient, if not comfortable.

TYPES OF FUEL

CHARCOAL   This type of fuel comes in two forms: lump and briquet. Lump charcoal is easier to light and burns faster. Briquets seem to be cleaner to handle and give a longer, more even heat performance.

WOOD   If available, it is an excellent source of heat, with hardwoods or fruitwoods giving the best flavor.

WOOD CHIPS   For an interesting smoky flavor, soak hardwood chips or fruitwood chips in water and drop on a bed of hot coals or hot wood.

TYPES OF IGNITERS

WADDED PAPER   Twist several "logs" of newspaper and place charcoal or wood over them; light a match to the paper.

COMMERCIAL PRODUCTS   These include gels, fluids, and tablets that are specially formulated to light fires easily. Keep containers away from the heat of the grill to avoid accidents.

ELECTRIC RODS   Merely plug this fire-starter into an outdoor socket and nestle the rod into the heap of charcoal until the fuel ignites.

154

TOOLS AND ACCESSORIES

Asbestos gloves
Basting brush
Black iron skillet
Bottle of water, water gun, or can of sand (to control flames)
Chafing dishes (heated by electricity or alcohol)
Electric coffee maker
Electric rotisserie unit
Electric warming tray
Grill brush and cleaner
Heavy-duty aluminum foil
Kabob skewers
Large apron
Long-handled knife, fork, spoon, turner, and tongs
Long-handled two-sided racks (for broiling small items
    together)
Potholders
Wooden board for slicing

ACKNOWLEDGEMENTS

Deep appreciation and grateful thanks to the following companies for their valued assistance during the preparation of this book:

Accent International   The Aluminum Association   American Lamb Council   American Molasses Company   The Broiler Council   Campbell Soup Company   Diamond Walnut Growers   Duffy-Mott Company   Florida Citrus Commission   R. T. French Company   Frito-Lay Inc.   General Foods Inc.   Green Giant Company   Hunt-Wesson Company   Instant Potato Products Association   International Shrimp Council   Kellogg Company   La Choy Food Products   Nestle Company   Ocean Spray Cranberries Inc.   Oscar Mayer & Company   Pineapple Growers Association   Processed Apple Institute   Rice Council   Riviana Foods Inc.   S & W Fine Foods   J. M. Smucker Company   Sun Maid Raisin Growers   Swift & Company   Tabasco Company   Tuna Council   Underwood Company   United Fruit Company

Index